REVISED *and* UPDATED!

2 EDITION

BOOKS THAT CH*A*NGE LI*V*ES

Recommended Reading Lists for Christian Readers

CLC PUBLICATIONS
Fort Washington, PA 19034

THE**parable**GROUP®

Books That Change Lives

© 2014 by CLC Publications in association with The Parable Group

Published by CLC Publications

U.S.A.
P.O. Box 1449, Fort Washington, PA 19034

UNITED KINGDOM
CLC International (UK)
51 The Dean, Alresford, Hampshire, SO24 9BJ

Books That Change Lives: Recommended Reading Lists for Christian Readers © 2005 by Parable Press.

Printed in the United States of America

Cover Design by Kevin Watson, The Parable Group.

First Edition (paperback): 2005 ISBN-10: 0-9770565-0-3
Second Edition (paperback): 2014 ISBN-13: 978-1-61958-171-5
Second Edition (e-book): 2014 ISBN-13: 978-1-61958-172-2

Table of Contents

Introduction

"When I read, it's a chance to sit down with a great thinker or a great historian or an adventurer—or even an apostle—and absorb their wisdom. I don't know how many historians and philosophers I will ever have a chance to meet in this life and I certainly won't meet an apostle, but through great books, a reader has a chance to gain immeasurably from the experience and counsel of those more gifted. Good books are great road maps for life."

—Joni Eareckson Tada

Introducing the Personal Growth Library

Each of us can gain so much from reading the works of great Christian writers. We encourage you to start your own library of classics that have changed lives and offered inspiration to readers through the ages.

To help you begin your library, we have compiled a carefully selected list of recommended books, chosen for their depth of wisdom and their power to transform hearts and lives. Retail book experts, members of The Parable Group nationwide, gave us their best recommendations from years of listening to reader feedback and watching firsthand the impact of these books on lives.

Our prayer is that this guide may assist you in building a personal library to deepen your walk with God, as well as help you choose books to lend to others so they can do the same.

Chapter 1

Personal Growth Library

AUTHORS

A *to* C

Thomas á Kempis (Classic)
The Imitation of Christ
Is it the right time in your spiritual walk to read this great classic? Written five centuries ago by a humble monk, this timeless message of faith in Christ's teachings remains a vital source of spiritual strength for people seeking to follow in the footsteps of the Lord.

Randy Alcorn
Heaven
Have you ever wondered what heaven is really like? You may be astonished. In the most comprehensive and definitive book on heaven to date, Randy invites you to picture heaven the way Scripture describes it—a bright, vibrant and physical new earth, free from sin, suffering and death and brimming with Christ's presence, wondrous natural beauty and the richness of human culture as God intended it.

Samuel Bagster (Classic)
Daily Light on the Daily Path
As Anne Graham Lotz describes in her introduction, this devotional is a spiritual baton to be passed down from generation to generation. It contains daily devotions, readings from the New King James Version for every morning and evening, and a topical index of sixty subjects including love, hope, salvation, forgiveness and baptism.

Randy Alcorn

Randy Alcorn is a former pastor and the founder and director of Eternal Perspective Ministries (EPM), a nonprofit organization dedicated to teaching biblical truth and drawing attention to the needy. EPM exists to meet the needs of the unreached, unfed, unborn, uneducated, unreconciled and unsupported people around the world.

"My ministry focus is communicating the strategic importance of using our earthly time, money, possessions and opportunities to invest in need-meeting ministries that count for eternity," Alcorn says. "I do that by trying to analyze, teach and apply the implications of Christian truth."

Alcorn is the author of more than forty books, including the best sellers *Heaven*, *The Treasure Principle*, *Deadline* and the Gold Medallion winner, *Safely Home*. His books in print exceed seven million and have been translated into over thirty languages.

What five books (other than the Bible) have had the largest impact on your life?

- *The Knowledge of the Holy* by A.W. Tozer
- *Mere Christianity* by C. S. Lewis
- *Systematic Theology* (or the condensed version, *Bible Doctrine*) by Wayne Grudem
- *The Chronicles of Narnia* by C. S. Lewis
- *Desiring God* by John Piper

James M. Boice (Classic)
Foundations of the Christian Faith
In one systematic volume, James Boice provides a readable overview of Christian theology. Students and pastors alike will benefit from this rich source that covers all the major doctrines of Christianity with scholarly rigor and a pastor's heart.

Dietrich Bonhoeffer (Classic)
The Cost of Discipleship
One of the most important theologians of the twentieth century unflinchingly considers what the demands of sacrifice and ethical consistency mean to people today. "Cheap grace," Bonhoeffer wrote, "is the grace we bestow on ourselves. Costly grace is the Gospel."

Edward M. Bounds (Classic)
Power Through Prayer
Pastor and civil war chaplain E. M. Bounds penned his slim classic on prayer for the simple reason that Christians don't pray enough. "The little estimate we put on prayer is evident from the little time we give to it," he wrote. "Talking to men for God is a great thing, but talking to God for men is greater still."

Jerry Bridges
The Discipline of Grace
Bible teacher Jerry Bridges invites Christian believers who are pursuing holiness to pause and consider the role of God's grace in making such pursuit possible. He urges the discernment of grace and the subsequent practice of the disciplines of commitment, conviction and more.

Jerry Bridges
The Practice of Godliness
Scripture says God has given us "everything we need for life and godliness," but what makes a Christian godly? Bridges examines what it means to grow in Christian character and helps us establish the foundation upon which that character is built.

Tony Evans

Dr. Tony Evans is one of the country's most respected evangelical leaders. He is a pastor, best-selling author, and frequent speaker at conferences and seminars across the nation. Through his church, Oak Cliff Bible Fellowship in Dallas, Texas, and his national ministry, The Urban Alternative, Dr. Evans has initiated a philosophy of ministry that teaches God's comprehensive rule over every area of life, demonstrated through the individual, family, church and society. He is the author of many books, including the best-selling *Kingdom Man* and *Kingdom Woman*.

What five books (other than the Bible) have had the largest impact on your life and why?

- *Eternal Destiny* by Jody (Joseph) Dillow presents a comprehensive discussion of soteriology, the part of theology concerned with our salvation through the death of Christ.

- *Ordering Your Private World* by Gordon McDonald helped me in generating very deep spiritual introspection.

- *Balancing the Christian Life* by Charles Ryrie presents the key elements for living the Christian life in a very succinct way.

- *Black and Free* by Tom Skinner helped set a foundation for me on the Kingdom agenda and race.

- *Experiencing God* by Henry Blackaby assisted in moving me from simply looking at God theologically to experiencing Him relationally.

Jerry Bridges
The Pursuit of Holiness

God commands His people: "Be holy, for I am holy." Does holiness seem unattainable? You'll discover how God has equipped you to live a holy life as Bridges clarifies what we should rely on God to do and what we should accept as our own responsibility.

Jerry Bridges
Trusting God

When hard times hit, God's sovereignty can be a comfort instead of a conundrum. *Trusting God* explores the scope of God's power over nations, nature and the detailed lives of individuals and helps us discern God's loving control. As we come to know Him better, we will trust Him more completely.

> **Excerpt from *The Practice of Godliness* by Jerry Bridges**
> "Any time we stress the personal responsibility of practical actions...we are in danger of thinking that the pursuit of holiness does depend upon our own willpower, our own strength of character. Nothing is further from the truth. We are both personally responsible and totally dependent in our practice of godliness. We cannot change our hearts; that is the exclusive work of the Holy Spirit. But we can and must avail ourselves of the means he uses." [1]

Brother Andrew (Classic)
God's Smuggler

As a boy, Brother Andrew dreamed of being an undercover spy. As a man, he found himself working undercover for God, smuggling Bibles into countries against incredible odds. Here is the amazing and inspiring true story of what God can do through a man of prayer.

Brother Lawrence (Classic)
The Practice of the Presence of God

For nearly 300 years, this unparalleled classic has given both blessing and instruction to those who can be content with nothing less than knowing God in all His majesty and feeling His loving presence throughout each simple day.

F. F. Bruce (Classic)
The New Testament Documents: Are They Reliable?
Because Christianity claims to be a historical revelation, says Bruce, the question of the reliability of the documents on which it was founded is a crucial one. Here he presents the most convincing evidence for the historical trustworthiness of the canon of the New Testament.

John Bunyan (Classic)
The Pilgrim's Progress
The classic drama of Christian's journey to discover eternal life offers readers encouragement and direction for their own pilgrimage. Bunyan captures the speech of ordinary people as accurately as he depicts their behavior and their inner emotional and spiritual life. The tale is spiced with Bunyan's acute and satirical perceptions of the vanity and hypocrisy of his own society.

Todd Burpo
Heaven is for Real
The true story of the four-year-old son of a pastor who, during emergency surgery, slips from consciousness and enters heaven. He survives and begins sharing the disarmingly simple message: Heaven is a real place, Jesus really loves children, and we must be ready for a coming last battle!

John Calvin (Classic)
The Institutes of the Christian Religion
Calvin's masterwork evokes strong emotions and has formed the church's understanding of Christian doctrine for generations, exerting untold influence in the development of Western thought. He enables readers to accurately handle the great doctrines and promises of the Bible.

Amy Carmichael (Classic)
If
Are you ready to risk going deeper for the Lord? Dare to read this little book about Calvary love lived out in common life, based on 1 Corinthians 13. Short, hard-hitting truths about the attitude of a follower of Christ will challenge you to the core, exhorting you to comprehend and embody the love shown on the cross.

Oswald Chambers (Classic)
My Utmost for His Highest
For nearly seventy five years, millions of Christians have trusted the spiritual companionship of Oswald Chambers' classic daily devotional. These brief Scripture-based readings—by turns comforting and challenging—will draw you into God's presence. You'll treasure their insight, still fresh and vital, and you'll discover what it means to offer God your very best for His greatest purpose—to truly offer Him your utmost for His highest.

Francis Chan
Crazy Love
God is calling you to a passionate love relationship with Himself. The answer to religious complacency isn't working harder at a list of do's and don'ts – it's falling in love with God. Once you encounter His love, as Francis describes it, you will never be the same. When you're wildly in love with someone, it changes everything.

Francis Chan
Forgotten God
Francis Chan rips away paper and bows to get at the true source of the church's power—the Holy Spirit. Chan contends that we've ignored the Spirit for far too long, and we are reaping the disastrous results. Thorough scriptural support and compelling narrative form Chan's invitation to stop and remember the One we've forgotten: the Spirit of the living God.

Francis Chan
Erasing Hell
How could a loving God send people to hell? Will people have a chance after they die to believe in Jesus and go to heaven? With a humble respect for God's Word, Francis Chan and Preston Sprinkle address the deepest questions you have about eternal destiny. As they write: "We cannot afford to be wrong on this issue."

Matt Chandler
The Explicit Gospel
In the Christian community, there's talk of Jesus and good deeds, but are we really entrenched in the gospel message? *The Explicit Gospel* is a wake-up call to unite the church and its believers to know and celebrate the gospel in its fullness.

Gary Chapman
The 5 Love Languages
This is the breakthrough book that reveals how people express love in different ways. By teaching us how to identify and use our spouse's preferred language when we express our love for him or her, Dr. Chapman shows us how wonderful things can happen to relationships.

Stephen Charnock (Classic)
The Existence and Attributes of God
Let this seventeenth century classic bring your twenty-first-century faith to a whole new level. Puritan theologian Stephen Charnock constructs an awe-inspiring portrait of God's attributes from theology and painstaking study of Scripture.

G. K. Chesterton (Classic)
Orthodoxy
Chesterton described this work as a "slovenly autobiography." His humility is admirable, since this work of intellectual clarity and literary skill describes his pilgrimage to belief that orthodox Catholic Christianity was the way to satisfy his personal emotional needs and live happily in society.

Henry Cloud
Boundaries
Having clear boundaries is essential to a healthy, balanced lifestyle. A boundary is a personal property line that marks those things for which we are responsible. In other words, boundaries define who we are and who we are not. Discover how boundaries impact all areas of our lives: physical, mental, emotional and spiritual.

Terri Blackstock

Terri is a *New York Times* best-selling author, with more than six million copies of her books sold worldwide. She is the winner of two Carol Awards, a Christian Retailers Choice Award, and a Romantic Times Book Reviews Career Achievement Award, among others.

During the first part of her career, Terri was an award-winning secular novelist writing for HarperCollins, Harlequin and Silhouette. Despite her success, she was miserable. Career compromises had taken their toll on her spiritual life, and she yearned to renew her relationship with Christ. After much soul-searching, Terri told the Lord that she would never again write a work that didn't glorify Him. She is now known for writing award-winning novels about Christians in crisis, primarily in the suspense genre.

Recent books include her acclaimed *Intervention* series. Other favorites include *Shadow in Serenity, Predator* and *Double Minds,* and the *Restoration* series, the *Newpointe 911* series, the *Cape Refuge* series, and the *SunCoast Chronicles* series.

Terri has been a guest on national television programs such as *The 700 Club, At Home Live with Chuck and Jenny* and *Home Life*, as well as numerous radio programs.

What five books (other than the Bible) have had the largest impact on your life?

- *This Present Darkness* by Frank Peretti
- *God's Covenant* by Kay Arthur
- *Mere Christianity* by C. S. Lewis

- *My Utmost for His Highest* by Oswald Chambers
- *Lord of the Rings Trilogy* by J. R. R. Tolkien

What is your goal for writing?

"My goal in writing Christian novels is to entertain my readers with a fast-paced page-turner, while teaching truths that are woven into the plot like a fine tapestry, truths that will point my readers to Christ or challenge them to a deeper walk with Him."–Terri Blackstock

---

Robert Coleman
The Master Plan of Evangelism
A classic for more than thirty years, this builds on the premise that Jesus' strategies for evangelism are still the best for outreach today. It shows you how following Christ's "master plan" can make you more effective at spreading the life-changing message of the gospel.

Charles Colson (Classic)
How Now Shall We Live?
Once we are transformed by a personal relationship with Jesus Christ, how do we go about transforming the world? This gives Christians the understanding, confidence and tools to confront bankrupt worldviews in this post-Judeo-Christian era, and restore and redeem every aspect of contemporary culture.

Excerpt from *The Master Plan of Evangelism* by Robert E. Coleman

"Having called his men, Jesus made it a practice to be with them. This was the essence of His training program—just letting His disciples follow Him. When one stops to think of it, this was an incredibly simple way of doing it. Jesus had no formal school, no Seminaries, no outlined course of study, no periodic membership classes in which He enrolled His followers. None of these highly organized procedures considered so necessary today entered at all into His ministry. Amazing as it may seem, all Jesus did to teach these men His way was to draw them close to Himself. He was His own school and curriculum." [2]

L. B. Cowman (Classic)
Streams in the Desert
Few books sustain such widespread recognition and perennial appeal. Cowman's devotional is a legacy of faith and wisdom that is refreshing, relevant and trustworthy in today's fast-paced world. Turn to it daily and let these prayerful writings lead you to the streams hidden beneath life's rocky terrain.

Jim Cymbala
Fresh Wind, Fresh Fire
Pastor Jim Cymbala shares the lessons he learned when the Spirit ignited his heart and began to move through the people at the Brooklyn Tabernacle. Transformed lives and the explosive growth of an amazing ministry will embolden you to pray for your own renewal.

Chapter 2

Personal Growth Library

AUTHORS

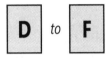

Kevin DeYoung
Crazy Busy: A (Mercifully) Short Book about a (Really) Big Problem
Is your life crazy busy? Drawing from personal struggles, DeYoung addresses
the problem of busyness and explains how a frantic life distracts from God's
purpose for us. DeYoung demonstrates how you can go from a prideful, con-
trolling state of busyness to trusting in God's providence and serving God
faithfully in life and ministry.

Kevin DeYoung
*Taking God at His Word: Why the Bible Is Knowable, Necessary, and
Enough, and What That Means for You and Me*
For centuries, the Bible has been under attack, and critics have questioned
its authority and inerrancy. In eight brief, easy-to-read chapters, DeYoung
provides a concise course in apologetics. Readers will come to understand
how Christians can trust Scripture and why that trust is essential to faith and
maturity in Christ.

Dr. James Dobson
Bringing Up Boys
Dr. James Dobson, the nation's most trusted parenting expert, offers sensible
advice and caring encouragement on raising boys. With so much confusion
about the role of men in our society, many of us are at a loss as to how to
bring up boys. Our culture has vilified masculinity and, as a result, boys are
suffering. Dobson tackles this issue with answers based on a firm foundation
of biblical principles.

Dr. James Dobson
Parenting Isn't for Cowards

This is the book frustrated parents have turned to for fifteen years. Why? Because Dr. Dobson, writing as a therapist and as a parent—and drawing on a landmark study of 35,000 patients—helps parents banish guilt, protect their sanity, restore their energy and enhance their relationships with their children.

Dr. James Dobson
The New Dare to Discipline

From one generation to the next, the challenge of helping children become responsible adults doesn't change. Dobson's reassuring guide for caring parents, first released in 1970, is now updated to help a whole new generation of parents with wise counsel.

Dr. James Dobson
The New Strong-Willed Child

Dr. Dobson has revised, updated and expanded his classic best seller for a new generation of parents and teachers. It incorporates the latest research on dealing with sibling rivalry, ADHD, low self-esteem and other important issues.

Henry Drummond (Classic)
The Greatest Thing in the World

The one great need in our Christian life is love—more love for God and more love for each other. This book will show you how to move into the "Love Chapter" of 1 Corinthians 13 and live there.

Gene Edwards
The Divine Romance

From the grandeur of creation to the glorious union of the Savior and His bride, God's majestic love sweeps through time, space and eternity in this greatest of all love stories.

Jonathan Edwards (Classic)
Religious Affections
Jonathan Edwards, the central figure in New England's first Great Awakening, presents a detailed description of the signs—true and false—of revival. He also dares to take a long, hard look at the evidence of true conversion and examines the controversial role emotions play in the Christian life.

Jonathan Edwards (Classic)
Sinners in the Hands of an Angry God
Theologian, missionary and pastor, renowned for the sermon for which the book is titled, Jonathan Edwards is considered by many historians to be the most brilliant American of his day. Explore the passionate New England preacher's penetrating spiritual insights in this attractively-bound collection of writings.

Jonathan Edwards (Classic)
Freedom of the Will
While *Sinners in the Hand of an Angry God* is his most famous work, many think *Freedom of the Will* is his best. Two-and-a-half centuries after Edwards wrote it, this book is still the most thorough argument for the complete sovereignty of God.

John Eldredge
Desire: The Journey We Must Take to Find the Life God Offers
Can desire really be from God? "The modern church," says John Eldredge, "mistakenly teaches its people to kill desire, calling it sin and replaces it with duty or obligation." The result? Christians tend to live safe, boring lives of resignation. This groundbreaking book invites readers to rediscover God-given desire, abandon resignation and embark on an adventure he calls, "our heart's most important journey."

John Eldredge
The Sacred Romance
Would you consider your relationship with God a romance? Too many believers today experience Christianity as a busyness-based religion and fail to understand that the God who saves us is also a God who woos us into a relationship of intimacy, beauty and adventure with Himself. Learn to identify the lies offered by "false loves" and journey back to the Lover of our souls.

Excerpt from *Desire* by John Eldredge

"Think for a moment. The One who created you and set all those loves and gifts in your heart, the One who has shaped all your life experiences (including the ones that seem to make no sense), this God has prepared a place for you that is a more than perfect fit for all your gifts and quirks and personality traits—even those you don't know you have. Christ is not joking when he says that we shall inherit the kingdom prepared for us and shall reign with him forever. We will take the position for which we have been uniquely made and will rule as he does—meaning with creativity and power."[3]

John Eldredge
Wild at Heart

"God designed men to be dangerous," says Eldredge. Simply look at the dreams and desires written in the heart of every boy: to be a hero, to be a warrior, to live a life of adventure and risk. Sadly, many men have buried their boyhood dreams and are often passive and bored to death. This trail-blazing book is helping men rediscover their God-given, masculine heart and releasing them to live bold lives for the glory of God.

Elisabeth Elliot
Passion and Purity

In this book on dating that has stood the test of time, Elisabeth Elliot teaches the often-painful yet rewarding discipline of waiting on God by candidly tracing her love story with Jim Elliot. Through letters, diary entries and memories, she shares the temptations, difficulties, victories and sacrifices of two young people whose commitment to Christ took priority.

Elisabeth Elliot
Shadow of the Almighty

This portrait of Jim Elliot, a rare and remarkable man of faith, is drawn from his rich and revealing diaries, tracing the roots of his commitment to God, even when he knew he might be called to an unexpected death in the prime of life. His martyrdom in 1956 shocked the nation and motivated thousands to a life of service.

Elisabeth Elliot
Through Gates of Splendor
The unforgettable true story of five men who sacrificed their lives to reach the Aucas with the gospel. This edition includes a follow-up chapter that will give readers a unique perspective on the mysterious ways God works to perform His wonders!

Francois Fénelon (Classic)
The Seeking Heart
The name Fénelon has stood for spiritual depth and insight for 300 years. Seeking Christians throughout the years have turned again and again to his writings for guidance and help in their quest for a deeper walk with Christ. Here are his works and letters for those who have a seeking heart.

Richard Foster
Celebration of Discipline
If you're spiritually thirsty, this may be the water you're seeking. Discover the deep rewards of cultivating the inward disciplines of meditation, prayer, fasting and study; the outward disciplines of simplicity, solitude, submission and service; and the corporate disciplines of confession, worship, guidance and celebration.

Richard Foster
Devotional Classics
Fifty-two selections introduce you to the world's great devotional writers through the course of one year. Each reading is accompanied by an introduction and meditation by Richard Foster, with discussion questions and more.

John Foxe (Classic)
Foxe's Book of Martyrs
With millions of copies in print, this classic of magnificent courage and faith traces the roots of religious persecution. This streamlined edition presents Foxe's work in today's language, commemorating the spiritual heroism of John Wycliffe, William Tyndale, Lady Jane Grey and many others.

Chapter 3
Personal Growth Library

AUTHORS

Elizabeth George
A Woman After God's Own Heart

As your daily duties nudge up against each other like cars in a traffic jam, are the needs of your soul pushed aside? Elizabeth George shows you how to gracefully coordinate your busy life by pursuing God's priorities first. This is a book for any woman who wants to achieve a growing relationship with God, develop an active partnership with her husband and make her home into a spiritual oasis.

Jim George
A Man After God's Own Heart

As a devoted Christian, passionate speaker, and prolific author, Jim George has taught, counseled and mentored men from all walks of life. He explains that a man's heartfelt desire to grow spiritually is all that's needed—God's grace does the rest. The reader will find encouragement to make lasting changes to his marriage, work and witness—putting God on display in his life and words.

Louie Giglio
I Am Not But I Know I AM

Dynamic communicator Louie Giglio puts success back into perspective. When John the Baptist said that he must decrease while Jesus must increase, he was expressing the secret to astonishing freedom—and incredible rest. Discover the rich, meaningful lifestyle of being small and you'll radiate the power of the God who is all the things you aren't.

Bob Goff
Love Does

Discover paradigm shifts, musings and stories from one of the world's most delightfully engaging people. What fuels his impact? Love. But it's not the kind of love that stops at thoughts and feelings. Bob's love takes action. Bob believes "Love Does." When "Love Does," life gets interesting—and this is one life you don't want to miss.

Billy Graham
Angels

The world continues to be fascinated with angels…but what does the Bible say about them? With more than a million copies sold, *Angels* gives ringing assurance that we are assisted and defended by a powerful order of invisible beings.

Billy Graham
Peace With God

With quiet confidence and sure-footed faith, Billy Graham points toward the One who is the only dependable source of peace that surpasses understanding. Both comforting and challenging, *Peace With God* has been changing lives for generations with chapters such as, "After Death—What?," "Hope for the Future" and "Peace at Last."

Billy Graham
The Journey: How to Live by Faith in an Uncertain World

Billy Graham is respected and loved around the world. This work is the culmination of a lifetime of experience and ministry. Graham leads us on a journey in faith, with insight that can only come from a life spent with God. *The Journey* is filled with wisdom, encouragement, hope and inspiration for anyone who wants to live a happier, more fulfilling life.

Billy Graham
The Reason for My Hope

At the age of ninety-five, Billy Graham proclaims God's gospel with resolve and deep compassion. It is a message he has been preaching for more than seventy years. In this book, you will sense its urgency, filled with hope for the future. Salvation is what we all long for, when we are lost, in danger, or have made a mess of our lives. Salvation belongs to us when we reach out for the only One who can rescue us—Jesus.

Wayne Grudem
Systematic Theology
Gain a solid understanding of the doctrines of the Christian church. This introductory textbook has several distinctive features: a strong emphasis on the scriptural basis for each doctrine; clear writing, with technical terms kept to a minimum; and a contemporary approach.

William Gurnall (Classic)
The Christian in Complete Armour (A three-volume set)
David Wilkerson, a seasoned veteran of spiritual warfare against the forces of darkness, writes: "I believe *The Christian in Complete Armour* should be in the library of every man and woman of God. No Christian leader, teacher, pastor, evangelist or worker should be without it."

Jeanne Guyon (Classic)
Experiencing the Depths of Jesus Christ
At one time this book was publicly burned in France, and yet it has played a major part in the lives of more famous Christians than perhaps any other Christian book. It is still thought by many to be one of the most helpful and powerful Christian books ever written.

Barbara Hughes
Disciplines of a Godly Woman
Using poignant stories and faithful reminders, Barbara opens her own heart to help you find the joy of full surrender. Her honest and encouraging look at the Word of God reveals the keys to living a truly godly life. To strengthen your walk day to day, she offers hymns and praise psalms for your devotional times, recommended books that will lift your spirits, and Bible study helps to remind you that you're not alone.

R. Kent Hughes
Disciplines of a Godly Man

For every man who wants to know what it means to be a Christian in today's world, this newly revised edition offers a frank biblical discussion on family, godliness, leadership, ministry and more, using engaging illustrations, scriptural wisdom, practical suggestions and study questions.

Hannah Hurnard (Classic)
Hinds' Feet on High Places

One of Hannah Hurnard's best-known and best-loved books, this allegory dramatizes the yearning of God's children to be led to new heights of love, joy and victory. Readers rejoice as Much-Afraid reaches the High Places, transformed by her union with the loving Shepherd.

> **Excerpt from *Hinds' Feet on High Places* by Hannah Hurnard**
> "The third thing that I learned was that you, my Lord, never regarded me as I actually was, lame and weak and crooked and cowardly. You saw me as I would be when you had done what you promised and had brought me to the High Places, when it could be truly said, 'There is none that walks with such a queenly ease, nor with such grace, as she.' You always treated me with the same love and graciousness as though I were a queen already and not wretched little Much-Afraid." [4]

Bill Hybels
Becoming a Contagious Christian

Learn how to share your faith in a natural, authentic way with others who need God's love and truth. This proven action plan will show you how to impact the spiritual lives of friends, family members, coworkers and others.

Bill Hybels
Just Walk Across the Room

Believers universally affirm that evangelism is a vital part of what God calls them to do, but very few make a practice of doing it. Drawing on fresh perspectives from Hybels' own experiences, as well as time-tested and practical illustrations, this book encourages and equips readers to routinely initiate spiritual conversations with those who don't know Christ.

Bill Hybels
Too Busy Not to Pray
We always mean to pray, but responsibilities and relationships can distract us. Pastor Bill Hybels reminds us these commitments should actually drive us to our knees. The ACTS formula (Adoration, Confession, Thanksgiving and Supplication) helps us rediscover the power and passion of prayer.

Kyle Idleman
Not a Fan
Are you a follower of Jesus? Consider this book a 'Define the Relationship' conversation to determine exactly where you stand. You may be a passionate, fully devoted follower of Jesus. Or, you may be just a fan who admires Jesus but aren't ready to let him cramp your style. Then again, maybe you're not into Jesus, period. In any case, don't take the question lightly.

Timothy Keller
The Prodigal God
Keller takes his trademark intellectual approach to understanding Christianity and uses the parable of the prodigal son to reveal an unexpected message of hope and salvation. Within that parable, Jesus reveals God's prodigal grace toward both the irreligious and the moralistic. This book will challenge both the devout and skeptics to see Christianity in a whole new way.

Timothy Keller
The Reason for God
Timothy Keller addresses the frequent doubts that skeptics and nonbelievers bring to religion. Using literature, philosophy, anthropology, pop culture and intellectual reasoning, Keller explains how the belief in a Christian God is, in fact, a sound and rational one. To true believers he offers a solid platform on which to stand against the backlash toward religion spawned by the Age of Skepticism.

Timothy Keller
Walking with God through Pain and Suffering
Here is the definitive Christian book on why bad things happen and how we should respond to them. The question of why there is pain and suffering in

the world has confounded every generation; yet there has not been a major book from a Christian perspective exploring why they exist for many years.

W. Phillip Keller (Classic)
A Shepherd Looks at Psalm 23
Because Keller was once a shepherd, God used his experience to give him these remarkable insights into Psalm 23. Discover the expressions of love that Christ, the Great Shepherd, extends to us, "the sheep of His pasture."

James Gilchrist Lawson (Classic)
Deeper Experiences of Famous Christians
How did famous Christians of the ages reach their mountaintop experiences of God's love and power? John Bunyan, Fénelon, Madame Guyon, D.L. Moody and many others reveal their intimate spiritual lives.

C. S. Lewis (Classic)
A Grief Observed
Written after his wife's tragic death, as a way of surviving the "mad midnight moment," *A Grief Observed* is a beautiful and unflinchingly honest record of how even a stalwart believer can lose all sense of meaning in the universe and then gradually regain his bearings.

C. S. Lewis (Classic)
Mere Christianity
Unavoidably logical and relentlessly persuasive, this intellectual introduction to Christianity uncovers common ground upon which all Christians can stand together. This forceful and accessible discussion of Christian belief has become one of the most popular introductions to Christianity and one of Lewis' most popular books.

C. S. Lewis (Classic)
Miracles
Who would have thought logic could prove miracles? C. S. Lewis uses his remarkable intellect to build a solid argument for the existence of divine intervention. This is his impeccable inquiry into the proposition that supernatural events can happen in this world.

C. S. Lewis (Classic)
The Space Trilogy
Lewis' acclaimed *The Space Trilogy* includes: *Out of the Silent Planet, Perelandra* and *That Hideous Strength.* The remarkable Dr. Ransom is abducted by a maniacal physicist and taken via spaceship to the red planet of Malacandra to be a human sacrifice. He escapes and becomes a stranger in a land enchantingly different from Earth, yet instructively similar.

C. S. Lewis (Classic)
Surprised by Joy
Lewis is a philosopher who thought his way to God. As an acutely perceptive observer of self, Lewis vividly recounts his spiritual journey, describing his early schooldays, his World War I experiences and his life at Oxford where he was drawn to God in a convergence of the rational and the spiritual.

C. S. Lewis (Classic)
The Abolition of Man
Lewis challenges public education by addressing a broad sweep of political, religious and philosophical concerns with razor-sharp intellect and wit. The modern god of relativism is forced to bow his knee to Lewis' exaltation of truth and universal values.

C. S. Lewis (Classic)
The Chronicles of Narnia
Once you enter the magical kingdom of Narnia through the back of a humble wardrobe, you will never want to come out again until you've experienced all seven grand adventures! The Narnia stories are allegories of the great truths of the Christian faith embedded in stories that have delighted and stirred hearts for many generations.

C. S. Lewis (Classic)
The Great Divorce
Lewis exposes mankind's pathetic reasons for refusing the Lord's grace-filled invitation to enter heaven. The players in this imaginative allegory create clear portraits of human self-deception and leave an indelible memory of hell's vast loneliness and heaven's vast freedom.

C. S. Lewis (Classic)
The Problem of Pain
It's the universal question: Why must humanity suffer? For ourselves and for those who ask us, thank heaven for this thoughtful work by C. S. Lewis. He honestly confronts pain and suffering and provides an answer to this critical theological problem.

C. S. Lewis (Classic)
The Screwtape Letters
How does the devil think? How does he tempt, blind and fool Christians? In this humorous and perceptive exchange between two devils, C. S. Lewis imparts a better understanding of how the enemy works and what it means to live a faithful life.

C. S. Lewis (Classic)
The Weight of Glory
Selected from sermons delivered by C. S. Lewis during World War II, these nine sermons offer guidance and inspiration in a time of great doubt, address increasing faith in any generation, and provide a compassionate vision of Christianity.

C. S. Lewis (Classic)
Till We Have Faces: A Myth Retold
This tale of two princesses—one beautiful and one unattractive—and the struggle between sacred and profane love is Lewis' reworking of the myth of Cupid and Psyche and one of his most enduring works.

Paul E. Little (Classic)
Know What You Believe
A Christian's faith must be grounded in truth so they can mature in God and produce the fruit of the Spirit. This is a classic, trusted resource on the fundamental doctrines of Christianity for new believers and longtime Christians.

Paul E. Little (Classic)
Know Why You Believe

After we develop some understanding of what we believe as Christians, we can have many questions. How can I know that there is a God? Did Jesus really rise from the dead? Why is there pain and evil in the world? This book will help you find the answers.

Martyn Lloyd-Jones (Classic)
Studies in the Sermon on the Mount

A spiritual classic, this comprehensive study by one of the greatest expository preachers of our time explains the Sermon on the Mount and applies it to the Christian life. Vastly rich truths are gleaned for the reader's spiritual growth, and great depth of thought is expressed in simple language.

Max Lucado
Grace for the Moment

For such a small book, *Grace for the Moment* has had a major impact on countless lives. With well over a million copies sold, this devotional continues to touch lives as it emphasizes the help and hope of God in everyday moments. Each daily reading features devotional writings from Max Lucado's numerous best sellers as well as a Scripture verse selected especially for that day's reading.

Max Lucado
In the Grip of Grace

Can anything separate us from the love of God? Can you drift too far? Wait too long? Out-sin the love of God? The answer is found in one of life's sweetest words—grace. Max Lucado shows how you can't fall beyond God's love.

Max Lucado
Just Like Jesus

God loves you just the way you are…but He refuses to leave you that way. Why? Because our ultimate goal should be a life that is just like Jesus. With determination, faith and God's help, we can all change for the better, no matter how long we have practiced our bad habits.

Max Lucado

With over 82 million books sold worldwide in more than forty-one languages, Max Lucado has touched millions with his signature writing style.

Max's books have made every major national best seller list. He is the first author to win the Gold Medallion Christian Book of the Year three times—1999 for *Just Like Jesus*, 1997 for *In the Grip of Grace* and 1995 for *When God Whispers Your Name*. In 1994, he became the only author to have eleven of his twelve books in print simultaneously appear on paperback, hardcover and children's CBA best seller lists.

In addition to his nonfiction books, Max has authored several award winning children's titles, including *Just In Case You Ever Wonder, The Crippled Lamb, Alabaster's Song* and the award-winning *You Are Special*. He also served as the general editor for the best-selling *Devotional Bible* and *God's Inspirational Promise Book*.

Featured in countless national media outlets, Max was dubbed "America's Pastor" by *Reader's Digest,* and named one of the most influential leaders in social media by the *New York Times*.

Max is the Preaching Minister at Oak Hills Church in San Antonio, Texas.

What books (other than the Bible) have had the largest impact on your life?

- *The Singer* by Calvin Miller
- *Growing Strong in the Seasons of Life* by Charles R. Swindoll
- *Peculiar Treasures* by Frederick Buechner
- *Mere Christianity* by C. S. Lewis

What can you share that would encourage someone else to read more?

"Readers catch writers at their best."

Max Lucado
You'll Get Through This
Max Lucado reminds readers that God doesn't promise that getting through trials will be quick or painless. With the compassion of a pastor, the heart of a storyteller, and the joy of one who has seen what God can do, Max explores the story of Joseph and the truth of Genesis 50:20. What Satan intends for evil, God redeems for good.

Martin Luther (Classic)
Luther's Small Catechism with Explanation
Considered "the layman's Bible," *Luther's Small* and *Large Catechisms* contain "everything which…a Christian must know for his salvation." Rich with Luther's vivid language, this contemporary *New International Version* translation includes an appendix, a description of Lutheran confessional writings and a topical index.

Erwin Lutzer

Dr. Erwin W. Lutzer is Senior Pastor of the Moody Church in Chicago. A graduate of Dallas Theological Seminary and Loyola University, he is the author of more than twenty books, including the Gold Medallion award-winner *Hitler's Cross* and the best seller *One Minute After You Die*.

Erwin is a teacher on radio programs heard on more than 700 stations throughout the United States and the world, including *The Moody Church Hour, Songs in the Night*, and *Running to Win*. He and his wife, Rebecca, live in the Chicago area and have three married children and seven grandchildren.

What five books (other than the Bible) have had the largest impact on your life?

- *The Bondage of the Will* by Martin Luther
- *The Adversary* by Mark Bubeck
- *The Pleasures of God* by John Piper
- *Desiring God* by John Piper
- *Whatever Happened to the Human Race* by Francis Schaeffer

Chapter 4

Personal Growth Library

AUTHORS

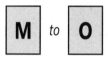

M *to* O

John MacArthur
Twelve Ordinary Men
Contrary to popular belief, we do not have to be perfect to do God's work. Look no further than the twelve disciples whose many weaknesses are forever preserved throughout the pages of the Bible. Jesus chose ordinary men and turned their weakness into strength, producing greatness from utter uselessness. MacArthur draws principles from Christ's careful, hands-on training of the original twelve disciples for today's modern disciple.

Brennan Manning (Classic)
Abba's Child: The Cry of the Heart for Intimate Belonging
Many Christians feel broken and angry but don't think they can express these real feelings around others – or to God. They put on a mask and hide from the One who truly loves them. Brennan Manning encourages readers to let go of the stressful, unreal impostor lifestyle and freely accept their identities as beloved children of God.

Brennan Manning (Classic)
Ruthless Trust
How do we overcome our fears and doubts? "Learn to trust God," says Manning, "and be more fully open to the promise of divine love. If we unite our faith and hope, the yield is greater trust in God." Written in the refreshingly honest tone that made *The Ragamuffin Gospel* so successful and readable, Manning leads his readers to the next level, calling on them to

shed the limitations of fear, shame and doubt and put their trust in God's unconditional love.

Brennan Manning (Classic)
The Ragamuffin Gospel
Many believers agonize over failures and pull away from God because they believe He is disappointed in them. In this repackaged edition—now with full appendix, study questions and the author's epilogue—Manning shows that nothing could be further from the truth.

Walter Martin (Classic)
The Kingdom of the Cults
Since 1965, this is the leading reference work on the major contemporary cult systems. With substantial new information evaluating each cult's history and contrasting their teaching with true biblical theology, it is essential in dealing with cults at home and overseas.

Eric Mason
Manhood Restored: How the Gospel Makes Men Whole
What does it mean to be a man? From broken homes to social evils, the definition of manhood has been corrupted and the perception of masculinity is skewed. By looking to Jesus as the ultimate standard for manhood, Mason provides theological insight into the restoration of men and their transformation to a life God has always intended for them—self-sacrificing, humble, fearless servants of God.

Josh McDowell
More Than a Carpenter
Josh McDowell used to argue persuasively and passionately against Jesus. Now he argues persuasively and passionately for Him and can help you to do the same. This hard-hitting book will help you talk with people who are skeptical about Jesus' divinity, His resurrection and His claims on their lives.

Robert McGee
The Search for Significance
In this relaunch of the timeless, two million-selling classic, you will gain new skills for getting off the performance treadmill, discover how four false beliefs

have negatively impacted your life, and learn how to overcome obstacles that prevent you from experiencing the truth of self-worth.

Eric Metaxas
Bonhoeffer: Pastor, Martyr, Prophet, Spy
As Hitler seduced a nation and attempted to exterminate the Jews of Europe, a small number of saboteurs worked to dismantle the Third Reich from the inside. One of these was Dietrich Bonhoeffer—a pastor and author. Eric Metaxas takes both strands of Bonhoeffer's life—the theologian and the spy —and draws them together to tell a searing story of incredible moral courage in the face of monstrous evil.

Donald Miller
Blue Like Jazz
In this intimate, soul-searching account, Miller describes his remarkable journey back to a culturally relevant, infinitely loving God. For anyone wondering if the Christian faith is still relevant in a postmodern culture, or anyone thirsting for a genuine encounter with a God who is real, *Blue Like Jazz* is a fresh and original perspective on life, love and redemption.

Paul E. Miller
A Loving Life: In a World of Broken Relationships
What is love? How do you create a community united in love? Through the story of Ruth, Miller provides a biblical model for love that enriches our understanding of God's love and the gospel. Miller offers hope to modern widows and to those who have suffered broken relationships. Discover how true love is rooted in God and His Word.

Paul E. Miller
A Praying Life: Connecting with God in a Distracting World
Prayer is a fundamental part of our communion with God. But how often do we get on our knees other than to ask God to bless the food at mealtimes or heal our sick bodies? Miller teaches the necessity of prayer for daily life and encourages us to commit to a prayerful and joyous life.

Andrew Murray (Classic)
Abide in Christ
Murray believed many Christians hesitate at the door of God's throne room

instead of accepting God's invitation to come in. He knew what it meant to be continually in the Father's presence and in these thirty-one heart-searching readings based on John 15, he shares how to live in fellowship with Jesus.

Andrew Murray (Classic)
Absolute Surrender
Do you yearn to delight in the fellowship of Jesus and discover victory over sin? First published more than a century ago, this book has allowed thousands to discover that victory and unbroken fellowship with Jesus are only a step away.

Andrew Murray (Classic)
Humility
This frank discussion of humility was written by a man qualified to write it. He admits his pride was so great that he tried to stop a revival for which his father had prayed for sixty years! God ultimately taught Murray humility and its relation to faith, holiness and happiness, and he shares it all in this book.

Andrew Murray (Classic)
With Christ in the School of Prayer
Prepare yourself for intercessory prayer. Using Jesus' teaching on prayer as a model, Murray expounds on the secret of believing in prayer, the certainty of answered prayer, the power of prevailing prayer and the chief end of prayer. This special revised edition includes a time line of history and an illustrated biography.

Iain H. Murray (Classic)
David Martyn Lloyd-Jones: The Fight of Faith 1939-1981
This volume begins as the ministry of Martyn Lloyd-Jones at Westminster Chapel suddenly changes. His hard work during the war years becomes foundational to his great influence in London and eventually in even wider circles: universities, Europe, America, South Africa—and through his books, to the whole world.

Iain H. Murray (Classic)
David Martyn Lloyd-Jones: The First Forty Years 1899-1939
The events that moved Martyn Lloyd-Jones from a glamorous Harley Street medical practice to a pastorate in an impoverished Welsh mining town make intriguing and inspiring reading.

Kyle Idleman

Kyle Idleman is the Teaching Pastor at Southeast Christian Church located in Louisville, Kentucky with over 22,000 in attendance every weekend. He is the best-selling author of *Not a Fan* and *Gods at War* as well as author and presenter of numerous video curriculums. Kyle's favorite thing to do is hang out with the love of his life, DesiRae. They have been married for seventeen years and have four children: MacKenzie, Morgan, Macy and Kael.

What five books (other than the Bible) have had the largest impact on your life and why?

- *As One Without Authority* by Fred Craddock: It helped me think outside of the box about preaching.

- *The Homiletical Plot* by Eugene Lowry: It took me even further outside the box and made preaching something I not only loved to do, but something I really enjoyed, too.

- *In the Name of Jesus* by Henri Nouwen: It is a leadership book like no other, and it warrants reading over and over.

- *Missional Church*, edited by Darrell Guder: It changed the way I think about church, and I am still learning from reading it almost five years ago.

- *God on Fire* by Fred Hartley: It is challenging me to encounter the presence of Jesus more radically.

Watchman Nee (Classic)
The Normal Christian Life
What is the normal Christian life? Starting from key passages in Romans, Nee reveals the secret of spiritual vitality that should be the normal experience of every Christian. His emphasis on the blood and the cross of Jesus Christ illustrates how we should live out the gospel: "I live no longer, but Christ lives His life in me."

Watchman Nee (Classic)
Spiritual Authority
The chapters in this volume on the nature of spiritual authority are drawn from a series of messages delivered by the great Chinese preacher-teacher, Watchman Nee, during a training period for Christian workers in China in 1948.

Watchman Nee (Classic)
Sit, Walk, Stand
Watchman Nee simplifies Ephesians into memorable and practical statements based on three key ideas: Our position in Chrisst is one of sitting, our life in the world is one of walking, and our attitude toward Satan is one of standing. "We do not fight for victory, we fight from victory."

Watchman Nee (Classic)
The Spiritual Man
For more than seventy years, *The Spiritual Man*, Watchman Nee's classic on spiritual growth, has helped believers advance in their pursuit of gaining Christ by showing them the way to let the Lord fully gain them. He emphasizes clear guidance on the proper path so that all those who seek after God with an honest heart can go step by step accordingly.

Henri Nouwen (Classic)
The Return of the Prodigal Son: A Story of Homecoming
The lessons are many in this powerful drama of fatherhood, filial duty, rivalry and anger between brothers, and they are all eloquently taught by this beloved spiritual writer. As he meditates in writing on this parable, he fluently imparts its enduring lessons for believers.

Stormie Omartian
The Power of a Praying Wife

Today's challenges and pressures can make a fulfilling marriage seem like an impossible dream, yet God delights in doing the impossible if only we would ask. Stormie Omartian shares how God has strengthened her own marriage since she began to pray for her husband concerning key areas of his life.

Stormie Omartian
The Power of a Praying Woman

It may seem easier to pray for your spouse, your children, your friends and your extended family, but God wants to hear your requests for your life too. He loves it when you come to Him for the things you need and ask Him to help you become the woman you have always longed to be.

Stormie Omartian
The Power of a Praying Parent

After decades of raising her children along with her husband, Michael, Stormie looks back at the trials, joys and power found in praying for her kids. In thirty easy-to-read chapters, she shares from personal experience how parents can pray for their children's safety, character, friends, relationship with God and more.

Excerpt from *The Power of a Praying Wife* by Stormie Omartian

"When we live by the power of God rather than our flesh, we don't have to strive for power with our words. 'For the kingdom of God is not in word but in power' (1 Corinthians 4:20). It's not the words we speak that make a difference, it is the power of God accompanying them. You'll be amazed at how much power your words have when you pray before you speak them. You'll be even more amazed at what can happen when you shut up and let God work." [5]

Chapter 5

Personal Growth Library

AUTHORS

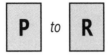

P *to* **R**

J. I. Packer
Evangelism and the Sovereignty of God
The seeming paradox between evangelism and God's sovereignty has been causing disagreements and confusion among Christians since the beginning of the twentieth century. By debunking the erroneous view that these doctrines are foes rather than friends, Packer adeptly moves through the obstacle course of tricky theology with ease and grace, allowing the reader a more complete understanding of the mystery of salvation.

J. I. Packer
Knowing God
The apostle Paul counted everything in his life as rubbish in comparison with knowing Jesus Christ. In this updated and revised edition of Packer's classic, you will discover the difference between knowing God and knowing about Him.

J. B. Philips (Classic)
Your God Is Too Small
In a world expanded to the point of bewilderment by global events and scientific discoveries, our idea of God must expand beyond "Resident Policeman," "Grand Old Man," "Managing Director" or any of the other small, inadequate boxes we try to fit Him into.

Arthur W. Pink (Classic)
The Attributes of God

"Tell me a little about yourself!" Friendships and job interviews begin with this invitation. In these pages, Pink tells us wondrous things about the Lord—His characteristics and attributes—so we can meet our greatest personal and salvational need—to truly, thoroughly know and love God.

Arthur W. Pink (Classic)
The Sovereignty of God

In many modern books, especially those that address the issue of pain and calamity, the subject of God's ultimate control is addressed. This is a classic on the subject of sovereignty, honoring God with His proper place of supremacy.

John Piper
A Godward Life

One hundred twenty vignettes focus on the radical consequences of living with God at the center of all we do. Steeped in Scripture, this is a passionate and articulate call for believers to live in conscious and glad submission to the sovereignty and glory of God.

> **Excerpt from *Knowing God* by J. I. Packer**
>
> "It is a staggering thing, but it is true—the relationship in which sinful human beings know God is one in which God, so to speak, takes them on to his staff, to be henceforth His fellow-workers (see 1 Cor 3:9) and personal friends. The action of God in taking Joseph from prison to become Pharaoh's prime minister is a picture of what he does to every Christian: from being Satan's prisoner, he finds himself transferred to a position of trust in the service of God. At once, his life is transformed. Whether being a servant is matter for shame or for pride depends on whose servant one is." [6]

John Piper

ECPA Gold Medallion winner John Piper is chancellor of Bethlehem College & Seminary and founder and teacher of desiringGod.org. He grew up in Greenville, South Carolina, and studied at Wheaton College, where he first sensed God's call to enter ministry. He went on to earn degrees from Fuller Theological Seminary (B.D.) and the University of Munich (D.Theol.).

For six years, John taught Biblical Studies at Bethel College in St. Paul, Minnesota, and in 1980, he accepted the call to serve as senior pastor at Bethlehem Baptist Church in Minneapolis, Minnesota, where he served for over thirty years.

John is the author of more than fifty books including *When I Don't Desire God*, *Desiring God*, *Don't Waste Your Life*, *A Hunger for God* and *The Passion of Jesus Christ*. His preaching and teaching is featured on the daily radio program *Desiring God*.

What books (other than the Bible) have had the largest impact on your life?

- *Hermeneutics* by Daniel Fuller
- *The Unity of the Bible* by Daniel Fuller
- *Validity in Interpretation* by E. D. Hirsch
- *How to Read a Book* by Mortimer Adler and Charles Van Doren
- *Mere Christianity* by C. S. Lewis

- *The Screwtape Letters* by C. S. Lewis
- *The Lion, the Witch and the Wardrobe* by C. S. Lewis
- *Freedom of the Will* by Jonathan Edwards
- *A Dissertation Concerning the End for Which God Created the World* by Jonathan Edwards
- *The Presence of the Future* by George Ladd

John Piper
Desiring God

In this paradigm-shattering classic, newly revised and expanded, John Piper reveals that the debate between duty and delight doesn't truly exist: Delight is our duty. Readers will embark on a dramatically different and joyful experience of their faith.

John Piper
Don't Waste Your Life

It's easy to slip through life without taking any risks—without making your life count. But life is short and precious; it shouldn't be wasted. You don't need to know a lot to make a lasting difference in the world, but you do have to know the few great, unchanging and glorious things that matter—and be willing to live and die for them.

David Platt
Follow Me

What did Jesus really mean when he said, "Follow me"? Platt contends that multitudes of people around the world culturally think they are Christians yet biblically are not followers of Christ. *Follow Me* explores the gravity of what we must forsake in this world, as well as the indescribable joy and deep satisfaction to be found when we live for Christ. It's a summons to lose your life—and to find new life in Christ.

David Platt
Radical
It's easy for American Christians to forget how Jesus said His followers would live and what their new lifestyle would actually look like. They would, He said, leave behind security, money, convenience, even family for Him. They would abandon everything for the gospel. Platt challenges you to hear what Jesus actually said about being His disciple and invites you to "believe" and "obey" what you have heard.

Leonard Ravenhill (Classic)
Why Revival Tarries
Appalled by the disparity between the New Testament church and the church today, Leonard Ravenhill, one of the twentieth century's greatest authorities on revival, sounded a no-compromise call to believers. His message is drastic, fearless, often radical and as timely as when it was published nearly fifty years ago.

Don Richardson
Peace Child
How do you communicate the gospel to cannibalistic people who not only condone cruelty and treachery, but honor them as ideals? Determined to find a way, the Richardsons approached the Sawi tribe in 1962, armed only with the story of God's "Peace Child." This book is a gripping account of God's faithfulness.

Karen Kingsbury

Karen Kingsbury is America's favorite inspirational novelist, with several of her titles debuting at or near the top of the *New York Times* best sellers list. She is also a public speaker, reaching more than 100,000 women annually through various national events. Karen lives and works outside Nashville, Tennessee, with her husband, Don, and their five sons, three of whom were adopted from Haiti. Their only daughter, Kelsey, is an actress in inspirational films and married to Christian recording artist Kyle Kupecky.

What five books (other than the Bible) have had the largest impact on your life and why?

- *Redeeming Love* by Francine Rivers: Before reading this book, I didn't feel called to write Christian fiction. I wanted to write about difficult, real-life topics and I didn't think that could happen in the Christian fiction genre. Then I read *Redeeming Love*, and as I finished the last page I hit my knees. I apologized for ever thinking that writing for God would somehow be second best. I asked Him to use me and my gift of storytelling for His purposes all the days of my life.

- *Deadline* by Randy Alcorn: Again, I didn't realize a Christian novel could be so powerful. I read this book before I wrote my first novel and it impacted me in a way that has remained. Reading Randy's novel made me realize that true and life-changing fiction involves four parts—the physical story, the intellectual story, the emotional story and the spiritual story. I knew I could never do anything less.

- *The Pursuit of Holiness* by Jerry Bridges: I became a Christian later in life, at age twenty-three. Because of that I had and still have a hunger for how to live for God. *The Pursuit of Holiness* spoke straight to my soul and helped me see what living for God looked like. I highlighted it and underlined it and read it over and over again.

- *How The Grinch Stole Christmas!* by Dr. Seuss: I was five years old when my parents gave me the hardback copy of *The Grinch*. I read it so many times I memorized it. I was very young but something stirred in my heart and I absolutely knew I would be a storyteller all the days of my life. I wrote my first book that year. *The Horse* was a simple story about a girl named Karen whose best friend was a horse named "Horse." It didn't have a very developed plot and the crayon-colored words slanted down every page. But the experience of *The Grinch* changed my life.

- *The Screwtape Letters* by C. S. Lewis: After giving my life to the Lord, I found the wonders of the most amazing author in C. S. Lewis. My husband and I did a Bible study through our church and the focus was this book. It forever helped me to know how the enemy of our souls is likely thinking. It helps me remember that life is a battle and I want always to be mindful of how desperately I need Jesus and His Spirit.

Fritz Ridenour
So What's the Difference?
Have you ever wondered what the difference is between orthodox biblical Christianity and other faiths? Revised and updated to help Christians better understand their own beliefs, this 1967 explanatory classic offers straightforward, noncritical comparisons of the basic tenets of the major world religions.

Frances Roberts (Classic)
Come Away My Beloved
Be swept away by God's love. *Come Away My Beloved* ministers encouragement, hope, comfort and conviction to both new Christians and long-time believers seeking spiritual renewal, leading you deeper into devotion to the Lord.

Paul Miller

After cofounding a multiracial inner city Christian school in Philadelphia, Paul helped his father (Jack Miller) start World Harvest Mission, where he served as associate director for fourteen years. During that time, he wrote the Sonship Course. In 1999, he founded seeJesus, an international discipling mission focused on helping the church see the person of Jesus. He has written three books: *A Praying Life* (2009), *A Loving Life* (2014), and *Love Walked Among Us* (2001) along with multiple discipling courses. His passion is writing interactive Bible studies that make Scripture come alive. He and his wife, Jill, have six children and nine grandchildren.

What five books (other than the Bible) have had the largest impact on your life and why?

- *The Cross of Christ* by John Stott: Stott opened my eyes to a non-Stoic God, the passionate God of the Bible that I knew and loved.

- *The Wonder of Being* by Charles Malik: This book saved my soul in college. I've read it five times since then. It is a critique of Kant, but that is just what I needed because I'd so inhaled the spirit of the Enlightenment. Malik cuts through Kant's pretentiousness with a winsome humility. His critique of the modern soul read me like a book.

- *The Life and Times of Jesus the Messiah* by Alfred Edersheim: No book changed my life more than this book. I read it during a sabbatical—more like devoured it—over a three month period of time in 1991. I encountered Jesus like I never had before. I realized that I'd read the New Testament backwards, reading the Gospels through a Romans lens instead of reading Romans through a Gospels lens. Edersheim was the first modern evangelical intellectual to see the Person of Jesus – specifically Jesus' Jewishness. I'm sure that is because he grew up as an Orthodox Jew so he knew the Talmud and Mishnah well.

- *The Person and Work of Christ* by B. B. Warfield: Warfield's essay, "The Emotional Life of our Lord" gave me permission to see Jesus as a person. His sermon "Imitating the Incarnation" remapped my life.

- *Repentance and 21st Century Man* by Jack Miller (currently available as *Repentance: A Daring Call to Real Repentance*): My dad's emphasis on grace and repentance is seared on my soul.

J. C. Ryle (Classic)
Holiness
With his trademark candor, J. C. Ryle strips away the pious ornamentation that many confuse for holiness and unfolds the true beauty of being made holy by God. The first unabridged edition in decades, it includes a foreword by D. Martyn Lloyd-Jones and an exhaustive index of Scripture.

Charles Ryrie (Classic)
Basic Theology
Wouldn't it be wonderful to understand theology without all the jargon associated with it? Dr. Ryrie strips down the heavy terms to the simple language of explanation and arrives at certainty. This is, after all, the purpose of scriptural doctrine: " ... so that you may know that you have eternal life" (1 John 5:13).

Personal Growth Library

AUTHORS

Saint Augustine (Classic)
The City of God
One of the great cornerstones in the history of Christian philosophy, *The City of God* provides an insightful interpretation of the development of modern Western society and thought. Contrasting earthly and heavenly cities, Augustine explores human history in its relation to all eternity.

Saint Augustine (Classic)
Confessions
Augustine's autobiography is a moving and profound record of a human soul. The most widely read of all his works, it reveals both his struggles with faith and his love for his Master. He speaks to the heart of humanity about our weakness and frailty, our depravity and our need for a holy God.

J. Oswald Sanders (Classic)
Spiritual Leadership
Be motivated to press on in service for Jesus Christ and place your talents and powers at God's disposal, so you can become a leader used for His glory. In modern language, this classic illustrates biblical leadership principles and helps to apply them.

CHAPTER 6

Francis Schaeffer (Classic)
Escape from Reason
Many today are without God and sinking into despair, escaping into a fantasy world of experience, drugs and pornography. In this highly original book, Dr. Schaeffer traces the roots of the humanistic reasoning now blossoming in our literature, art and music, theater and cinema, television and popular culture.

Francis Schaeffer (Classic)
How Should We Then Live?
As one of the foremost evangelical thinkers of the twentieth century, Francis Schaeffer long pondered the fate of declining Western culture, analyzed the reasons for modern society's state of affairs and presented the only viable alternative: Living by the Christian ethic and accepting the Bible's morals, values and meaning.

Francis Schaeffer (Classic)
The Mark of a Christian
Bumper stickers are great, but Christians are supposed to be known by their love. Schaeffer confronts the not-so-pretty picture of Christianity sometimes presented to the world and challenges: "The world has turned away. Is there then no way to make the world look again—this time at true Christianity?"

Francis Schaeffer (Classic)
The God Who Is There
Where did the clashing ideas about God, science, history and art come from and where are they going? For over thirty years, this landmark book has changed the way the church sees the world, demonstrating how Christianity can confront the competing philosophies around the globe.

Francis Schaeffer (Classic)
True Spirituality
A treasure trove of wisdom for Christians trying to discover what true spirituality looks like in everyday life! Celebrate the thirtieth anniversary of this twentieth-century spiritual classic with a special commemorative edition featuring a foreword by Chuck Colson.

Francine Rivers

New York Times best-selling author Francine Rivers has published numerous novels—all best sellers—and she has continued to win both industry acclaim and reader loyalty around the globe. Her Christian novels have been awarded or nominated for many honors, including the RITA Award, the Christy Award, the ECPA Gold Medallion and the Holt Medallion in Honor of Outstanding Literary Talent. In 1997, after winning her third RITA Award for inspirational fiction, Francine was inducted into the Romance Writers of America Hall of Fame. Francine's novels have been translated into over twenty different languages.

Five books that stand out in my memory:

- *In His Steps* by Charles Sheldon: I read this soon after becoming a Christian and it continues to challenge me to live to please Jesus and to follow in His steps.

- *The Screwtape Letters* by C. S. Lewis: This book opened my eyes to spiritual warfare and how vulnerable we all are to attack. It reminds me to stay immersed in God's Word so that I will be able to recognize lies and hold fast to the truth.

- *A Christmas Carol* by Charles Dickens: Dickens' classic tale of the redemption of Scrooge is a masterpiece I never tire of reading or seeing on film every Christmas. No one is beyond hope.

- *Ben-Hur* by Lew Wallace: Wallace's classic tale of Christ brought biblical times and Rome to life.

- *East of Eden* by John Steinbeck: Last, but equal in quality, is Steinbeck's novel, the (perhaps unintentional) retelling of the Adam, Cain and Abel story. Steinbeck is a master craftsman who evokes emotion through the readers' strong bonds with his gritty characters.

Dutch Sheets
Intercessory Prayer
Have you ever wondered if your prayers really count? Or why you never seem to get any answers? If so, *Intercessory Prayer* will provide hope and convince you that your prayers can indeed move heaven and earth.

Charles Sheldon (Classic)
In His Steps
This classic is the work of Christian fiction that coined the phrase, "What would Jesus do?" For the first time in their lives, Rev. Henry Maxwell and his congregation are forced to consider this question and its consequences. No one in town is left untouched by the results.

Bruce Shelley (Classic)
Church History in Plain Language
It's about time someone wrote a church history about people, not just "eras" and "ages." This taps the roots of the Christian family tree, combining authoritative research with a captivating style.

Hannah Whitall Smith (Classic)
The Christian's Secret of a Happy Life
Loved for nearly a century and a half, this modern classic has helped millions of believers realize their Creator has given them the strength and spirit to move beyond life's difficulties and attain the shining happiness that is Christianity's promise.

Ann Spangler
Praying the Names of God
Learn how to study and pray God's names by focusing each week on one of the primary names or titles of God. By incorporating the divine names and titles into your prayers—and learning about the biblical context in which the name was revealed—you'll gain a more intimate understanding of who God is and how he can be relied on in every circumstance of your life.

Ann Spangler
Women of the Bible
In this year-long devotional, Ann Spangler focuses on fifty-two remarkable women in Scripture—women whose struggles to live with faith and courage are not unlike your own. Vital and deeply human, the women in this book encourage us through their failures as well as their successes. You'll see how God acted in surprising and wonderful ways to draw them—and you—to himself.

R. C. Sproul
Chosen by God
Here is a clear scriptural case for the classic and often controversial Christian doctrine of predestination. Through this view of a truly sovereign God, readers will see how sinfulness prevents man from choosing God on his own. Instead, God must change people's hearts.

R. C. Sproul
Essential Truths of the Christian Faith
With the layperson in mind, Dr. Sproul offers a basic understanding of the Christian faith and brief explanations of biblical concepts every Christian should know, in language everyone can understand. Highlighted with homespun analogies and one hundred plus doctrines categorized under easy-reference headings.

Excerpt from *The Christian's Secret of a Happy Life* by Hannah Whitall Smith

"An old writer says, 'All discouragement is from the devil;' and I wish every Christian would take this as a motto and would realize that he must fly from discouragement as he would from sin. But if we fail to recognize the truth about temptation, this is impossible; for if the temptations are our own fault, we cannot help being discouraged. But they are not. The Bible says, 'Blessed is the man that endureth temptation'; and we are exhorted to 'count it all joy when we fall in to diverse temptations.' Temptation, therefore, cannot be sin; and the truth is, it is no more a sin to hear these whispers and suggestions of evil in our souls than it is for us to hear the wicked talk of bad men as we pass them on the street. The sin comes, in either case, only by our stopping and joining in with them." [7]

R. C. Sproul
The Holiness of God
Just when we relax into the embrace of grace, we tense up when we consider the awesome holiness of God. Sproul's classic, now expanded and updated, eases the tension between God's terrifying holiness and His comforting mercy.

R. C. Sproul
What's in the Bible
Theologian R. C. Sproul and best-selling author Robert Wolgemuth collaborate to present an overview of the entire Bible. The resulting road map highlights the essence of God's voice, activity and purpose throughout the Old and New Testaments in a thoroughly readable form.

Charles Haddon Spurgeon (Classic)
All of Grace
"Meet me in heaven" is Charles Spurgeon's invitation in *All of Grace*—a clear, simple explanation of God's absolutely free gift of salvation. The great Baptist minister, known as 'the prince of all preachers' explains the gospel with illustrations, stories and the plain truth of God's Word. This nineteenth-century classic—said to be his all-time best seller—is sure to encourage believers and seekers alike.

Charles Haddon Spurgeon (Classic)
Morning and Evening
For tens of thousands of Christians over the last century, this has served as their daily devotional guide through life's ups and downs.

> **Excerpt from *Morning and Evening* by Charles Haddon Spurgeon**
> "Are you mourning, believer, because you are so weak in the divine life: because your faith is so small and your love so feeble? Cheer up, for you have cause for gratitude. Remember that in some things you are equal to the greatest and most full-grown Christian. You are as much bought with blood as he is. You are as much an adopted child of God as any other believer. An infant is as truly a child of its parents as is the full-grown man. You are as completely justified, for your justification is not a thing of degrees: your little faith has made you every bit as clean." [8]

Charles Haddon Spurgeon (Classic)
The Treasury of David

Plunge into Spurgeon's great commentary on the book of Psalms and drink deeply of the living water. Every word of Spurgeon's own exposition is updated. "Hints to Preachers" is displayed in outline form for preachers, crossed-referenced to Spurgeon's numbered sermons to aid further study.

Miles Stanford (Classic)
The Green Letters

"Not I but Christ." That brief phrase reflects our complete dependency on Jesus for everything that the Christian life is about, from right standing with God, to spiritual growth, to personal well-being, to practical service. *The Green Letters* emphasizes both the doctrinal and experiential aspects of maturing in Christian living.

Roger Steer (Classic)
George Mueller: Delighted in God

Never once advertising or making known his financial needs—except in prayer to God—George Mueller housed and fed thousands of homeless children in England. This is the life story of the man who lived by prayer and faith alone.

John R. W. Stott (Classic)
Basic Christianity

Here's the nutshell we're always talking about. In this classic little book, Stott presents the fundamentals of Christianity and urges the non-Christian to consider the claims of Christ.

Alexander Strauch (Classic)
Biblical Eldership

Elders play a critical role in our churches, supporting the pastor and serving the congregation. This practical book explains the categories of eldership, the duties and qualifications and even their relationships with each other. Excellent for choosing the right people to serve in this capacity.

Lee Strobel
The Case for Christ
Using the dramatic scenario of an investigative journalist pursuing his story and leads, Strobel uses his experience as an award-winning reporter for the *Chicago Tribune* to interview experts about the evidence for Christ from the fields of science, philosophy and history.

Lee Strobel
The Case for a Creator
Has science discovered God? At the very least, it's giving faith an immense boost as new findings emerge about the incredible complexity of our universe. Lee Strobel reexamines the theories that once led him away from God. Through his compelling account, you'll encounter the mind-stretching discoveries from cosmology to DNA research that present astonishing evidence in *The Case for a Creator*.

Lee Strobel
The Case for Faith
This eagerly anticipated sequel to Lee Strobel's best-selling *The Case for Christ* finds the author investigating the nettlesome issues and doubts of the heart that threaten faith. Eight major topics are addressed, including doubt, the problem of pain and the existence of evil.

Richard Swenson, MD
Margin
Dr. Richard Swenson sees a steady stream of exhausted, hurting people coming into his office suffering from the societal epidemic of "living without margin." Here, he offers an overall strategy for health that involves contentment, simplicity, balance and rest.

Charles R. Swindoll
Intimacy with the Almighty
From his own personal journal, Charles Swindoll offers all-new insights to guide readers on a journey to intimacy with God. This keepsake book with an embossed, antique-looking cover includes pages in Swindoll's handwriting.

Joel Rosenberg

Joel C. Rosenberg is a *New York Times* best-selling author, producer and speaker. He is the founder of The Joshua Fund, and has worked as a communications advisor for a number of US and Israeli leaders, including Steve Forbes, Rush Limbaugh, Natan Sharansky and Benjamin Netanyahu. In 2008, he hosted the first Epicenter Conference in Jerusalem, drawing two thousand Christians who wanted to "learn, pray, give, and go" to do the Lord's work in Israel and the Middle East.

The son of a Jewish father and a Gentile mother, Joel is an evangelical Christian with a passion for making disciples of all nations and teaching Bible prophecy. A graduate of Syracuse University with a BFA in filmmaking, he is married, has four sons, and lives near Washington, DC.

Here are twelve books that absolutely changed my life:

- *Fear No Evil* by Natan Sharansky: The spell-binding true story of a Jewish dissident who spent nine years in a KGB gulag—a man who became one of my heroes.

- *From Beirut to Jerusalem* by Thomas Friedman: The riveting account of a *New York Times* reporter covering the Middle East that made me want to spend my whole life understanding the epicenter.

- *Bonhoeffer: Pastor, Martyr, Prophet, Spy* by Eric Metaxas: The brilliant biography of one of the most courageous pastors in the history of Germany, a man who stood for Christ during the reign of Hitler.

- *Night* by Elie Wiesel: The terrifying true account of a Jewish man sent to the Auschwitz death camp who lost his faith in God.

- *The Hiding Place* by Corrie ten Boom: The amazing true story of a godly Christian woman who not only survived a Nazi concentration camp but learned to forgive her captors because of Jesus' love for her.

- *Mere Christianity* by C. S. Lewis: The most penetrating explanation of what it means to be a true follower of Jesus Christ ever written, by a former atheist professor at Oxford and Cambridge at that.

- *Just As I Am* by Billy Graham: The inspiring true story of a North Carolina farm boy who grew up to preach the gospel to more people face-to-face than anyone in all of human history.

- *Born Again* by Charles Colson: The game-changing true story of President Nixon's "hatchet man," arrested during Watergate, and sent to prison, who found utter forgiveness and redemption through Christ.

- *God's Smuggler* by Brother Andrew: The true story of a man willing to risk his life to bring the Word of God to the enslaved people of Eastern Europe and the Soviet Union.

- *The Coming Peace in the Middle East* by Tim LaHaye: Long out of print but the most fascinating book about Bible prophecy (specifically Ezekiel 38 & 39) I have ever read, bar none.

- *The Testament* by John Grisham: The first novel I ever read that was both absolutely thrilling and spiritually inspiring, something I'd never imagined was possible before reading this book.

- *The Training of the Twelve* by A. B. Bruce: The greatest book on how to make disciples by a pastor and theologian no one has ever heard of.

"Christians who are not reading these and other books are cheating themselves of the greatest adventure stories of all time!" Joel Rosenberg

Charles R. Swindoll
Jesus: The Greatest Life of All

Jesus Christ is, without question, the most influential person in history. But who exactly is He? Beloved pastor and Bible teacher Charles Swindoll introduces you to the carpenter from Nazareth as you have never seen Him before in a fascinating biography, filled with biblical and historical insights.

Charles R. Swindoll
David: A Man of Passion & Destiny
What does it mean to be someone "after God's own heart?" David, Old Testament shepherd, king and psalmist, offers an answer in the shape of his own life. David's life offers hope to all of us. It shows that God can do extraordinary things through ordinary men and women.

Joni Eareckson Tada
Joni—An Unforgettable Story
In this award-winning classic of faith's triumph over adversity, Joni reveals the meaning of her life and the special ways God reveals His love. This 25th Anniversary Edition describes her life since the book's publication in 1976, including her marriage to Ken Tada and the expansion of her worldwide ministry.

Tullian Tchividjian
Jesus + Nothing = Everything
With extraordinary zeal and biblical insight, Tchividjian shares how the power of the gospel transformed his life. He provides a simple equation to proclaim Christ's sufficiency in every area of life. Experience relief, freedom and joy in the Lord Jesus Christ.

Corrie ten Boom (Classic)
The Hiding Place
Corrie ten Boom's wondrous story tells of God's ability to illuminate the dark recesses of despair and foster forgiveness in a wounded heart. Corrie's saga of surviving the Ravensbruck concentration camp and moving into a life of miraculous ministry is a story for all Christians for all time.

Joni Eareckson Tada

Joni Eareckson Tada is the founder and CEO of Joni and Friends International Disability Center. In 1967, a diving accident left Joni a quadriplegic in a wheelchair. During two years of rehabilitation, she learned how to paint with a brush between her teeth. Her highly-detailed fine art paintings and prints are sought after and collected.

Joni is a popular conference speaker in the US and overseas, and the author of more than fifty books. Her best-selling and award-winning works cover topics ranging from disability outreach to reaching out to God, and include her autobiography, *Joni* (also a feature film), and her newest book, *Joni & Ken: An Untold Love Story*. Joni has also written several children's books, including *Tell Me the Promises*, which received the Evangelical Christian Publishers Association's Gold Medallion and Silver Medal in 1997. Another children's book, *Tell Me the Truth* received the EP Gold Medallion.

Joni has hosted the short-feature radio program, "Joni and Friends," since 1982, and has been featured on several major news programs and in magazines such as *Christianity Today* and *World Magazine*.

She has been the recipient of several honorary degrees and awards, including: Gold Medallion Lifetime Achievement Award from the Evangelical Christian Publishers Association and Illinois Wesleyan University's Society of World Changers.

What five books (other than the Bible) have had the largest impact on your life?

- *The Reformed Doctrine of Predestination* by Loraine Boettner
- *Holiness* by Bishop J. C. Ryle
- *Grace Grows Best in Winter* by Margaret Clarkson
- *The Book of Common Prayer*
- *Knowing God* by J. I. Packer

W. Ian Thomas (Classic)
The Saving Life of Christ
Wherever you are in your spiritual growth, you can always go further. This book, with deep reverence for its subject, takes readers on a journey to discover the deeper meanings of the Christian life.

A. W. Tozer (Classic)
The Attributes of God
Inspirational reading at its best. The chapters of this book were originally sermons preached by Tozer. Whether spoken or written, his words "promote personal heart religion" among God's people. You will learn about ten attributes of God, including goodness, mercy and grace.

A. W. Tozer (Classic)
The Knowledge of the Holy
If the title intimidates you, you're not alone; however, these pages contain wonderful knowledge of the nature of God and how we can recapture a sense of His awesome majesty. Rejuvenate your prayer life, meditate more reverently, understand God more deeply and experience His presence in your daily life.

A. W. Tozer (Classic)
The Pursuit of God
In his own time, Tozer was called the "twentieth-century prophet." Winner of the ECPA Platinum Book Award, this book is perhaps his greatest legacy to the church. Let its seeds of wisdom take root in your spirit and bear fruit for God.

Paul David Tripp

Dangerous Calling: Confronting the Unique Challenges of Pastoral Ministry

Let's face it: ministry is hard. *Dangerous Calling* examines the spiritual unrest and turmoil in the life of the pastor and surrounding church community. Tripp offers a cure as he emboldens pastors, church leaders and members of the congregation to build a healthy spiritual life that is God-centered and grace-given.

Dennis Rainey

Dennis Rainey is the President and CEO of FamilyLife, a division of Campus Crusade for Christ, and serves on the Board of Directors for FamilyLife and Dallas Theological Seminary.

Dennis has received two Gold Medallion Awards from the Evangelical Christian Publishers Association. He has authored and coauthored more than two dozen books, including the best-selling *Moments Together for Couples* and *Staying Close*. He is also the senior editor of the HomeBuilders Couples Series®, which has sold over 2.5 million copies in forty-seven languages.

The daily host of the nationally syndicated radio program FamilyLife Today, Dennis has received the National Religious Broadcasters Radio Program of the Year Award twice.

Dennis holds a master's degree in biblical studies from Dallas Theological Seminary, and an honorary doctorate from Trinity Evangelical University and Divinity School in Deerfield, Illinois.

What books (other than the Bible) have had the largest impact on your life?

- *Humility: The Beauty of Holiness* by Andrew Murray
- *The 7 Habits of Highly Successful People* by Stephen Covey
- *The Chronicles of Narnia* by C. S. Lewis
- *The Princess & the Goblin* by George MacDonald

Chapter 6

- *The Knowledge of the Holy* by A.W. Tozer
- *The Seven Laws of Teaching* by John Milton Gregory
- *Spiritual Leadership* by J. Oswald Sanders
- *Experiencing God Workbook* by Henry Blackaby
- *The Pursuit of God* by A. W. Tozer
- *Quiet Talks on Prayer* by S. D. Gordon

Chapter 7

Personal Growth Library

AUTHORS

V *to* Z

Ann Voskamp
One Thousand Gifts

How do we find joy in the midst of deadlines, debt, drama and daily duties? What does the Christ-life really look like when your days are gritty, long— and sometimes even dark?" Ann invites you to embrace everyday blessings and embark on the transformative spiritual discipline of chronicling God's gifts.

Rick Warren
The Purpose Driven Life

Why am I here? What is my purpose? These are the most basic questions we face in life. Self-help books suggest that people should look within, at their own desires and dreams, but Rick Warren says the starting place must be with God and his eternal purposes for each life. Real meaning and significance come from understanding and fulfilling God's purposes for putting us on earth.

Thomas Watson (Classic)
All Things for Good

When Watson, along with two thousand other ministers, was ejected from the Church of England and exposed to hardship and suffering, he wrote this inspiring testimony of Romans 8:28 and God's ability to "work all things together for good."

Robin Lee Hatcher

Best-selling novelist Robin Lee Hatcher is the author of over seventy contemporary and historical novels and novellas. Her many awards include the Christy Award for Excellence in Christian Fiction, the RITA Award for Best Inspirational, RWA's Lifetime Achievement Award, the Carol Award, and the Inspirational Reader's Choice Award.

A frequent speaker to writers' and women's groups, Robin is a past president of Romance Writers of America, Inc., a professional writers' organization with more than 8,400 members worldwide.

In recognition of her efforts on behalf of literacy, Laubach Literacy International (now known as ProLiteracy Worldwide) created the Robin Award in her honor.

What five books (other than the Bible) have had the largest impact on your life?

- *Redeeming Love* by Francine Rivers
- *The Hiding Place* by Corrie ten Boom
- *Prison to Praise* by Merlin Carothers
- *Experiencing God* by Henry Blackaby
- *The Purpose Driven Life* by Rick Warren

Thomas Watson (Classic)
The Doctrine of Repentance

Thomas Watson does not mince words: "Persons are veiled over with ignorance and self-love . . . the devil does with them as the falconer with the hawk. He blinds them and carries them hooded to hell." Repentance is essential to true Christianity and no better guide on the subject can be found.

Donald S. Whitney (Classic)
Spiritual Disciplines for the Christian Life

The freedom to grow in godliness—to naturally express Christ's character through your own personality—is in large part dependent on a deliberate cultivation of the spiritual disciplines. Far from being legalistic, restrictive, or binding, as they are often perceived, the spiritual disciplines are actually the means to unparalleled spiritual liberty. So if you'd like to embark on a lifelong quest for godliness, this book will help you on your way.

Warren Wiersbe (Classic)
The Best of A.W. Tozer

These fifty-two favorite chapters compiled by Warren Wiersbe represent the major themes from Tozer's works, each one inspiring reflection and meditation. From his knowledge and pursuit of God come these excerpts of light to penetrate and illuminate the human heart.

David Wilkerson (Classic)
The Cross and the Switchblade

When a young preacher left the hills of Pennsylvania to come to New York City, little did the world know he was an arrow sent from God to pierce the hearts of New York teens trapped by drugs and gangs. Over 14 million copies of David Wilkerson's amazing story are in print. Make sure you own one of them!

Dallas Willard (Classic)
Renovation of the Heart

Dallas Willard addresses a critical question for today: Why are there so many Christians not growing closer to Christlikeness and still struggling with sinful strongholds? *Renovation of the Heart* establishes a foundational understanding of human nature and the process of bringing about change.

Dallas Willard (Classic)
The Divine Conspiracy
This renowned teacher and writer calls us back to the true meaning of Christian discipleship. Willard argues compellingly for the relevance of God to every aspect of our existence, showing the necessity of profound changes in how we view our lives and faith.

Dallas Willard (Classic)
The Spirit of the Disciplines
One of today's most brilliant Christian minds explains how practice of the spiritual disciplines will enable ordinary men and women to enjoy the fruit of the Christian life. It is the key to self-transformation for everyone who wants to be a disciple of Jesus.

Dallas Willard (Classic)
Hearing God
Being close to God means communicating with him—telling him what is on our hearts in prayer and hearing and understanding what he is saying to us. It is this second half of our conversation with God that is so important but that can also be so difficult. How do we hear his voice? The key, says Dallas Willard, is to focus not so much on individual actions and decisions as on building our personal relationship with our Creator.

Philip Yancey
Prayer
Yancey strikes a moving chord with this book that is filled more with yearning and wonder than it is with easy answers. Prayer, he writes, is our partnership with God, our chance to join forces with God's power to confront suffering and evil head-on. The key, Yancey writes, is that prayer is a window to knowing the mind of God, whose kingdom is entrusted to all of us frail, selfish people on earth.

Philip Yancey
The Jesus I Never Knew
Phil Yancey reveals the real Jesus beyond the stereotypes, offering a new and different perspective on His life and work, and ultimately, who He was and why He came. In this steady look at Christ's radical words, the author asks whether we are taking Jesus seriously enough.

John Ortberg

John Ortberg is the senior pastor at Menlo Park Presbyterian Church in Menlo Park, California, and previously served as teaching pastor at Willow Creek Community Church in Chicago, Illinois. He holds a Master of Divinity and doctorate degree in clinical psychology from Fuller Seminary.

He is the best-selling author of books on spiritual formation including *The Life You've Always Wanted*, *Know Doubt*, *The Me I Want to Be*, *Who Is This Man?* and many other titles. He has served on the Board of Trustees, and written for *Christianity Today*, and is a frequent contributor to *Leadership Journal*. John is also a member of the Board of Trustees for Fuller Seminary and the Dallas Willard Center for Spiritual Formation.

What five books (other than the Bible) have had the largest impact on your life?

- *The Spirit of the Disciplines* by Dallas Willard—easily the most life-impacting book I've ever read.

- *The Divine Conspiracy* by Dallas Willard

- *Mere Christianity* by C. S. Lewis

- *The Prince of Tides* by Pat Conroy (my favorite contemporary novel—Pat Conroy makes me want to write)

- *The Practice of the Presence of God* by Brother Lawrence

Philip Yancey

Philip Yancey is the Editor-at-Large for *Christianity Today* magazine, and holds graduate degrees in Communications and English from Wheaton College Graduate School and the University of Chicago.

Philip has written twenty books, with 15 million copies in print worldwide in thirty-five languages, including thirteen Gold Medallion Award-winners and two that were awarded the Christian Book of the Year—*What's So Amazing About Grace?* and *The Jesus I Never Knew.*

What five books (other than the Bible) have had the largest impact on your life?

- *Orthodoxy* by G. K. Chesterton truly brought me back to faith.

- *The Problem of Pain* by C. S. Lewis encouraged me to explore answers to my own questions on suffering.

- *Pilgrim at Tinker Creek* by Annie Dillard reconnected me to the natural world as a window to the Creator.

- *Brother to a Dragonfly* by Will Campbell got me thinking about my southern childhood and about grace.

- *Telling the Truth* by Frederick Buechner raised my sights on what writing can do.

What got you into writing and what now are your goals as an author?

"I was attending grad school at Wheaton College and pounding doors of the Christian organizations located there until Harold Myra gave me a chance as a cub reporter at Campus Life. I worked there ten years, learning to write on the job and then went freelance. I'll always be grateful that I started writing for young people, a most fickle readership. I never had a 'captive' audience and that's a good discipline.

"I think more in terms of my calling as an author than my goals. My calling is to represent the ordinary pilgrim encountering things like suffering, doubt, prayer, Jesus, spiritual growth, missions—and somehow coming to terms with them. I feel like an advocate, able to spend the time and reflection on these issues on behalf of my readers."

Philip Yancey
Vanishing Grace

Yancey has focused on the search for honest faith that makes a difference for a world in pain. In his previous book *What's So Amazing About Grace?* he issued a call for Christians to be as grace-filled in their behavior as they are in declaring their beliefs. In *Vanishing Grace* he explains that people inside and outside the church are still thirsty for grace. Grace can bring together Christianity and our post-Christian culture, inviting us to take a deep second look at why our faith matters and how to reignite its appeal to future generations.

Philip Yancey
What's So Amazing About Grace?

"If grace is God's love for the undeserving," asks Yancey, "then how are believers doing at lavishing grace on a world that knows far more of cruelty and unforgiveness than it does of mercy?" Through powerful stories, Yancey takes a probing look at what grace looks like in action.

Philip Yancey
Where Is God When It Hurts?

Winner of the Gold Medallion Award and an inspirational best seller for more than twenty years, this is now revised and updated to explore issues that have arisen during that time. With sensitivity and caring, Yancey helps us understand why we suffer and how to cope with our own pain and that of others.

Sarah Young
Jesus Calling
After years of writing in her prayer journal, missionary Sarah Young decided to "listen" to God, writing down whatever she believed He was saying to her. Gradually her journaling changed from monologue to dialogue writtenfrom Jesus' point of view. She knew her writings were not inspired as Scripture is, but they helped her grow closer to God. Others were blessed by her writings, until people all over the world were using her messages.

Ravi Zacharias
Can Man Live Without God
In this brilliant and compelling defense of the Christian faith, apologetics scholar and popular speaker Ravi Zacharias shows that how you answer questions about God's existence will impact your relationship with others, your commitment to integrity, your attitude toward morality and your perception of truth.

Ravi Zacharias
Jesus Among Other Gods
Ravi Zacharias contrasts the truth of Jesus with founders of Islam, Hinduism and Buddhism, compelling believers to share their faith with our postmodern world. He shows how the blueprint for life and death itself is found in a true understanding of Jesus and celebrates the power of Jesus Christ to transform lives.

Ravi Zacharias
Beyond Opinion
Ravi Zacharias was once sharing his faith with a Hindu when the man asked: "If the Christian faith is truly supernatural, why is it not more evident in the lives of so many Christians I know?" The question hit hard, and this book is an answer. Its purpose is to equip Christians everywhere to simultaneously defend the faith and be transformed by it into people of compassion.

Notes

1. Jerry Bridges, *The Practice of Godliness* (Colorado Springs, CO: Navpress, 1983, 1996), page 156.

2. Robert E. Coleman, *The Master Plan of Evangelism* (Grand Rapids, Michigan: Fleming H. Revell Company, 1963,1964), page 38.

3. Reprinted by permission of Thomas Nelson Inc., Nashville, TN., from the book entitled *The Journey of Desire* copyright date 2000 by John Eldredge. All rights reserved.

4. Hannah Hurnard, *Hinds' Feet on High Places* (Wheaton, Illinois: Living Books, Tyndale House Publishers, Inc.1975), page 241.

5. Taken from: *The Power of a Praying Wife*. Copyright © 1997 by Stormie Omartian. Published by Harvest House Publishers, Eugene, Oregon. Used by permission.

6. J. I. Packer, *Knowing God* (Downers Grove, Illinois: InterVarsity Press,1973), page 32.

7. Hannah Whitall Smith, *The Christian's Secret of a Happy Life* (Old Tappan, New Jersey: Spire Books,1942), page 87.

8. Charles Haddon Spurgeon, *Morning and Evening* (Hendrickson Publishers,1995), page 586.

Chapter 8

Personal Growth Library List
by Category

Apologetics

Bruce, F. F., *The New Testament Documents: Are They Reliable?*
DeYoung, Kevin, *Taking God at His Word*
Keller, Timothy, *The Reason for God*
McDowell, Josh, *More Than a Carpenter*
Strobel, Lee, *The Case for a Creator*
Strobel, Lee, *The Case for Christ*
Strobel, Lee, *The Case for Faith*
Zacharias, Ravi, *Jesus Among Other Gods*
Zacharias, Ravi, *Beyond Opinion*

Bible Study

Sproul, R. C., *What's in the Bible*
Swindoll, Charles, *David: A Man of Passion & Destiny*
Watson, Thomas, *All Things for Good*

Biography

Brother Andrew, *God's Smuggler*
Elliot, Elisabeth, *Shadow of the Almighty*
Elliot, Elisabeth, *Through Gates of Splendor*
Lewis, C. S., *Surprised by Joy*
Metaxas, Eric, *Bonhoeffer: Pastor, Martyr, Prophet, Spy*
Murray, Iain, *David Martyn Lloyd-Jones: The Fight of Faith*
Murray, Iain, *David Martyn Lloyd-Jones: The First Forty Years*
Richardson, Don, *Peace Child*
Steer, Roger, *George Mueller: Delighted in God*
Tada, Joni Eareckson, *Joni—An Unforgettable Story*
ten Boom, Corrie, *The Hiding Place*
Wilkerson, David, *The Cross and the Switchblade*

Christian Classics

á Kempis, Thomas, *The Imitation of Christ*
Brother Lawrence, *The Practice of the Presence of God*
Drummond, Henry, *The Greatest Thing in the World*
Edwards, Jonathan, *Sinners in the Hands of an Angry God*
Edwards, Jonathan, *Freedom of the Will*
Edwards, Jonathan, *Religious Affections*
Fénelon, François, *The Seeking Heart*
Foxe, John, *Foxe's Book of Martyrs*
Gurnall, William, *The Christian in Complete Armour, Three Volume Set*
Guyon, Jeanne, *Experiencing the Depths of Jesus Christ*
Luther, Martin, *Luther's Small Catechism with Explanation*
Murray, Andrew, *Absolute Surrender*
Murray, Andrew, *Humility*
Murray, Andrew, *With Christ in the School of Prayer*
Murray, Andrew, *Abide in Christ*
Ryle, J. C., *Holiness*
Sanders, J. Oswald, *Spiritual Leadership*
Saint Augustine, *The City of God*
Smith, Hannah Whitall, *The Christian's Secret of a Happy Life*
Spurgeon, Charles Haddon, *All of Grace*
Spurgeon, Charles Haddon, *The Treasury of David*
Tozer, A. W., *The Attributes of God*
Tozer, A. W., *The Knowledge of the Holy*
Tozer, A. W., *The Pursuit of God*
Wiersbe, Warren, *The Best of A. W. Tozer*

Christian Living

Bonhoeffer, Dietrich, *The Cost of Discipleship*
Bridges, Jerry, *The Discipline of Grace*
Bridges, Jerry, *The Practice of Godliness*
Bridges, Jerry, *The Pursuit of Holiness*
Bridges, Jerry, *Trusting God*
Bunyan, John, *The Pilgrims Progress*
Burpo, Todd, *Heaven is for Real*
Carmichael, Amy, *If*
Chan, Francis, *Crazy Love*

Chan, Francis, *Erasing Hell*
Chan, Francis, *Forgotten God*
Chandler, Matt, *The Explicit Gospel*
Cloud, Henry, *Boundaries*
Colson, Charles, *How Now Shall We Live?*
Cymbala, Jim, *Fresh Wind, Fresh Fire*
Edwards, Gene, *The Divine Romance*
Eldredge, John, *Desire: The Journey We Must Take to Find the Life God Offers*
Eldredge, John, *The Sacred Romance*
Eldredge, John, *Wild at Heart*
Foster, Richard, *Celebration of Discipline*
George, Elizabeth, *A Woman After God's Own Heart*
George, Jim, *A Man After God's Own Heart*
Giglio, Louie, *I Am Not But I Know I AM*
Goff, Bob, *Love Does*
Graham, Billy, *Peace With God*
Graham, Billy, *The Journey: How to Live by Faith in an Uncertain World*
Graham, Billy, *The Reason for My Hope*
Hughes, Barbara, *Disciplines of a Godly Woman*
Hughes, R. Kent, *Disciplines of a Godly Man*
Hybels, Bill, *Becoming a Contagious Christian*
Idleman, Kyle, *Not a Fan*
Keller, Timothy, *The Prodigal God*
Keller, Timothy, *Walking with God through Pain and Suffering*
Lawson, James Gilchrist, *Deeper Experiences of Famous Christians*
Lewis, C. S., *Mere Christianity*
Lewis, C. S., *Miracles*
Lewis, C. S., *The Abolition of Man*
Lewis, C. S., *The Problem of Pain*
Lewis, C. S., *The Weight of Glory*
LLoyd-Jones, Martyn, *Studies in the Sermon on the Mount*
Lucado, Max, *Just Like Jesus*
Lucado, Max, *You'll Get Through This*
Lucado, Max, *In the Grip of Grace*
MacArthur, John, *Twelve Ordinary Men*

Manning, Brennan, *Abba's Child: The Cry of the Heart for Intimate Belonging*

Manning, Brennan, *Ruthless Trust*

Manning, Brennan, *The Ragamuffin Gospel*

McGee, Robert, *The Search for Significance*

Miller, Donald, *Blue Like Jazz*

Miller, Paul E., *A Loving Life: In a World of Broken Relationships*

Nee, Watchman, *The Normal Christian Life*

Nee, Watchman, *Spiritual Authority*

Nee, Watchman, *Sit, Walk, Stand*

Nee, Watchman, *The Spiritual Man*

Nouwen, Henri, *The Return of the Prodigal Son: A Story of Homecoming*

Omartian, Stormie, *The Power of a Praying Woman*

Packer, J. I., *Knowing God*

Phillips, J. B., *Your God Is Too Small*

Piper, John, *A Godward Life*

Piper, John, *Desiring God*

Piper, John, *Don't Waste Your Life*

Platt, David, *Follow Me*

Platt, David, *Radical*

Ravenhill, Leonard, *Why Revival Tarries*

Saint Augustine, *Confessions*

Schaeffer, Francis, *How Should We Then Live?*

Schaeffer, Francis, *The Mark of a Christian*

Stanford, Miles, *The Green Letters*

Swenson, Richard, *Margin*

Swindoll, Charles, *Intimacy with the Almighty*

Swindoll, Charles, *Jesus: The Greatest Life of All*

Tchividjian, Tullian, *Jesus + Nothing = Everything*

Thomas, W. Ian, *The Saving Life of Christ*

Voskamp, Ann, *One Thousand Gifts*

Warren, Rick, *The Purpose Driven Life*

Whitney, Donald S., *Spiritual Disciplines for the Christian Life*

Willard, Dallas, *Renovation of the Heart*

Willard, Dallas, *The Divine Conspiracy*

Willard, Dallas, *The Spirit of the Disciplines*

Willard, Dallas, *Hearing God*
Yancey, Philip, *The Jesus I Never Knew*
Yancey, Philip, *Vanishing Grace*
Yancey, Philip, *What's So Amazing About Grace?*
Zacharias, Ravi, *Can Man Live Without God*

Church History

Shelley, Bruce, *Church History in Plain Language*

Church Life

Strauch, Alexander, *Biblical Eldership*
Tripp, Paul David, *Dangerous Calling*

Devotionals

Bagster, Samuel, *Daily Light on the Daily Path*
Chambers, Oswald, *My Utmost for His Highest*
Cowman, L. B., *Streams in the Desert*
Foster, Richard, *Devotional Classics*
Keller, W. Phillip, *A Shepherd Looks at Psalm 23*
Lucado, Max, *Grace for the Moment*
Roberts, Frances, *Come Away My Beloved*
Spangler, Ann, *Women of the Bible*
Spurgeon, Charles Haddon, *Morning and Evening*
Young, Sarah, *Jesus Calling*

Emotional Needs, Stress

DeYoung, Kevin, *Crazy Busy*

Evangelism

Coleman, Robert, *The Master Plan of Evangelism*
Hybels, Bill, *Just Walk Across the Room*
Packer, J. I., *Evangelism and the Sovereignty of God*

Fiction

Hurnard, Hannah, *Hinds' Feet on High Places*
Lewis, C. S., *The Great Divorce*

Lewis, C. S., *The Screwtape Letters*
Lewis, C. S., *Till We Have Faces: A Myth Retold*
Lewis, C. S., *The Chronicles of Narnia*
Lewis, C. S., *The Space Trilogy*
Sheldon, Charles, *In His Steps*

Grief and Comfort

Lewis, C. S., *A Grief Observed*
Yancey, Philip, *Where Is God When It Hurts?*

Men's Issues

Mason, Eric, *Manhood Restored: How the Gospel Makes Men Whole*

Other Religions

Martin, Walter, *The Kingdom of the Cults*
Ridenour, Fritz, *So What's the Difference?*

Parenting/Family

Chapman, Gary, *The Five Love Languages*
Dobson, Dr. James, *Bringing Up Boys*
Dobson, Dr. James, *Parenting Isn't for Cowards*
Dobson, Dr. James, *The New Dare to Discipline*
Dobson, Dr. James, *The New Strong-Willed Child*

Prayer

Bounds, Edward M., *Power Through Prayer*
Hybels, Bill, *Too Busy Not to Pray*
Miller, Paul E., *A Praying Life: Connecting with God in a Distracting World*
Omartian, Stormie, *The Power of a Praying Wife*
Omartian, Stormie, *The Power of a Praying Parent*
Sheets, Dutch, *Intercessory Prayer*
Spangler, Ann, *Praying the Names of God*
Yancey, Philip, *Prayer*

Single Life

    Elliot, Elisabeth, *Passion and Purity*

Theology

    Alcorn, Randy, *Heaven*

    Boice, James M., *Foundations of the Christian Faith*

    Calvin, John, *The Institutes of the Christian Religion*

    Charnock, Stephen, *The Existence and Attributes of God*

    Chesterton, G. K., *Orthodoxy*

    Graham, Billy, *Angels*

    Grudem, Wayne, *Systematic Theology*

    Little, Paul E., *Know What You Believe*

    Little, Paul E., *Know Why You Believe*

    Pink, Arthur W., *The Attributes of God*

    Pink, Arthur W., *The Sovereignty of God*

    Ryrie, Charles, *Basic Theology*

    Schaeffer, Francis, *Escape from Reason*

    Sproul, R. C., *Chosen by God*

    Sproul, R. C., *Essential Truths of the Christian Faith*

    Sproul, R. C., *The Holiness of God*

    Stott, John R. W., *Basic Christianity*

    Watson, Thomas, *Doctrine of Repentance*

Chapter 9

Life Issues Topical Resource List

What is a Life Issues Topical Resource List?

"A friend at work says she's thinking about getting an abortion. Is there a book to help me talk with her?"

"My child is struggling with pornography. How can I help him?"

"My sister wants to find a husband so badly. I just don't know what to say to her."

Where do you look for help when confronted with these types of difficult situations? The Life Issues Topical Resource List is your guide to resources that will help you find answers. Grouped by the needs most often mentioned by Christian retailers throughout the country, we believe these books change lives.

Abortion

Cradle My Heart: Finding God's Love After Abortion (Kim Ketola and Ruth Graham)

Forgiven and Set Free: A Post-Abortion Bible Study for Women (Linda Cochran)

Her Choice to Heal: Finding Spiritual and Emotional Peace After Abortion (Sydna Masse)

ProLife Answers to ProChoice Arguments (Randy Alcorn)

Tilly (Frank E. Peretti)

You're Not Alone: Healing Through God's Grace After Abortion (Jennifer O'Neill)

Abstinence / Purity

Almost Sex: 9 Signs You Are about to Go Too Far (or Already Have) (Michael DiMarco and Hayley DiMarco)

And the Bride Wore White: Seven Secrets to Sexual Purity (Dannah Gresh)

Every Single Man's Battle: Staying on the Path of Sexual Purity (Stephen Arterburn and Fred Stoeker)

Every Single Woman's Battle: Guarding Your Heart and Mind Against Sexual and Emotional Compromise (Shannon Ethridge)

Gift-Wrapped by God: Secret Answers to the Question "Why Wait?" (Linda Dillow and Lorraine Pintus)

If You Really Loved Me: 100 Questions on Dating, Relationships, and Sexual Purity (Jason Evert)

Passion and Purity: Learning to Bring Your Love Life Under Christ's Control (Elisabeth Elliot, Joshua Harris and Ruth Bell Graham)

Sex Has a Price Tag: Discussions about Sexuality, Spirituality, and Self Respect (Pam Stenzel, Rick Bundschuh and Steven Case)

Sex Is Not the Problem (Lust Is) (Joshua Harris)

Sexual Integrity [June Hunt Hope for the Heart]: Balancing Your Passion with Purity (June Hunt)

Sexy Girls: How Hot Is Too Hot? (Hayley DiMarco)

Technical Virgin: How Far Is Too Far? (Hayley DiMarco)

The Purity Code: God's Plan for Sex and Your Body (Jim Burns)

The Truth about Sex: What the World Won't Tell You and God Wants You to Know (Kay Arthur)

Abuse - Physical / Emotional / Self

A League of Dangerous Women: True Stories from the Road to Redemption (Mary Frances Bowley and James Lund)

Angry Men and the Women Who Love Them: Breaking the Cycle of Physical and Emotional Abuse (Paul Hegstrom)

Healing the Scars of Emotional Abuse (Gregory Jantz and Ann McMurray)

Inside a Cutter's Mind: Understanding and Helping Those Who Self-Injure (Jerusha Clark and Earl Henslin)

No Place for Abuse: Biblical & Practical Resources to Counteract Domestic Violence (Catherine Clark Kroeger and Nancy Nason-Clark)

Refuge from Abuse: Healing and Hope for Abused Christian Women (Catherine Clark Kroeger and Nancy Nason-Clark)

Self-Injury: When Pain Feels Good (Edward T. Welch)

ADD/ADHD

Adult AD/HD: A Reader Friendly Guide to Identifying, Understanding, and Treating Adult Attention Deficit/Hyperactivity Disorder (Thomas Whiteman and Michele Novotni)

The Link Between ADD and Addiction: Getting the Help You Deserve (Wendy Richardson)

When Too Much Isn't Enough: Ending the Destructive Cycle of Ad/HD and Addictive Behavior (Wendy Richardson and Eugene H. Peterson)

Addiction / Recovery

12 Steps F/Christians (Updated) (Friends in Recovery and Rpi)

Celebrate Recovery: A Recovery Program Based on Eight Principles from the Beatitudes (John Baker and Rick Warren)

Freedom from Addiction: Breaking the Bondage of Addiction and Finding Freedom in Christ (Neil T. Anderson, Mike Quarles and Julia Quarles)

Good News for the Chemically Dependent and Those Who Love Them (Jeff Vanvonderen)

Overcoming Addictive Behavior: The Victory Over the Darkness Series (Neil T. Anderson and Mike Quarles)

Seven Snares of the Enemy (Erwin W. Lutzer)

The Last Addiction: Own Your Desire, Live Beyond Your Recovery, Find Lasting Freedom (Sharon A. Hersh)

Tony Evans Speaks Out on Gambling (Tony Evans)

Adoption

A Treasury of Adoption Miracles: True Stories of God's Presence Today (Karen Kingsbury)

Adopted and Loved Forever (Annetta E. Dellinger and Janet McDonnell)

Carried Safely Home: The Spiritual Legacy of an Adoptive Family (Kristin Swick Wong)

Handbook on Thriving as an Adoptive Family: Real-Life Solutions to Common Challenges (David Sanford and Renee S. Sanford)

Questions Adoptees Are Asking: About Beginnings, about Birth Family, about Searching, about Finding Peace (Sherrie Eldridge)

Saving Levi: Left to Die, Destined to Live (Lisa Misraje Bentley)

Successful Adoption: A Guide for Christian Families (Natalie Nichols Gillespie)

Wounded Children, Healing Homes: How Traumatized Children Impact Adoptive and Foster Families (Jayne E. Schooler, Betsy Keefer Smalley and Timothy J. Callahan)

Aging

A Promise Kept (Robertson McQuilkin)

Green Leaves for Later Years: The Spiritual Path of Wisdom (Emilie Griffin)

Loving Your Parents When They Can No Longer Love You (Terry D. Hargrave)

Men in Midlife Crisis (Jim Conway)

Mid-Course Correction (Gordon MacDonald)

Nearing Home: Life, Faith, and Finishing Well (Billy Graham)

Alcoholism

Dying for a Drink: What You and Your Family Should Know about Alcoholism (Anderson Spickard, Jr. and Barbara R. Thompson)

God Is for the Alcoholic (Jerry G. Dunn and Bernard Palmer)

Sober Mercies: How Love Caught Up with a Christian Drunk (Heather Harpham Kopp)

Anger

Angry Teens and the Parents Who Love Them (Sandy Austin)

Mad about Us: Moving from Anger to Intimacy with Your Spouse (Gary J. Oliver and Carrie Oliver)

Overcoming Emotions That Destroy Study Guide: Practical Help for Those Angry Feelings That Ruin Relationships (Chip Ingram)

She's Gonna Blow! (Julie Ann Barnhill)

The Anger Trap: Free Yourself from the Frustrations That Sabotage Your Life (Les Carter and Frank B. Minirth)

Anxiety / Fear / Worry

Fear: No Longer Afraid (June Hunt)

Fearless (Max Lucado)

Freedom from Fear (Neil T. Anderson, Rich Miller and Julianne S. Zuehlke)

Go Away, Dark Night (Liz Curtis Higgs and Nancy Munger)

Helping Your Kids Deal with Anger, Fear, and Sadness (H. Norman Wright)

Just Enough Light for the Step I'm on: Trusting God in the Tough Times (Stormie Omartian)

Overcoming Fear, Worry, and Anxiety: Becoming a Woman of Faith and Confidence (Elyse Fitzpatrick)

The Anxiety Cure (Archibald D. Hart)

Be Not Afraid: A Disciple's Guide to Loving God and Others (David Ivaska)

The Worry Workbook: Twelve Steps to Anxiety-Free Living (Les Carter and Frank B. Minirth)

Apologetics

Beyond Opinion: Living the Faith We Defend (Ravi Zacharias and Danielle DuRant)

Can Man Live Without God (Ravi K. Zacharias)

Jesus Among Other Gods: The Absolute Claims of the Christian Message (Ravi K. Zacharias)

Know What You Believe: Connecting Faith and Truth (Paul E. Little)

Know Why You Believe (Paul E. Little and James F. Nyquist)

More Than a Carpenter (Josh McDowell and Sean McDowell)

The Case for a Creator: A Journalist Investigates Scientific Evidence That Points Toward God (Lee Strobel)

The Case for Christ: A Journalist's Personal Investigation of the Evidence for Jesus (Lee Strobel)

The Case for Faith: A Journalist Investigates the Toughest Objections to Christianity (Lee Strobel)

The New Testament Documents: Are They Reliable? (Frederick Fyvie Bruce and N. T. Wright)

The Reason for God: Belief in an Age of Skepticism (Timothy Keller)

Bible Study

All Things for Good (Thomas Watson)

David: A Man of Passion & Destiny (Charles R. Swindoll)

How to Read the Bible for All Its Worth (Gordon D. Fee and Douglas Stuart)

What's in the Bible: A One-Volume Guidebook to God's Word (R. C. Sproul and Robert Wolgemuth)

Cancer

Cancer: A Medical and Spiritual Guide for Patients and Their Families (William A. Fintel, Gerald R. McDermott and Dave Dravecky)

Everyday Strength: A Cancer Patient's Guide to Spiritual Survival (Randy Becton and Dave Dravecky)

Grace for Each Hour: Through the Breast Cancer Journey (Mary J. Nelson)

Hope in the Face of Cancer (Amy Givler and M. D. Givler)

Plant a Geranium in Your Cranium: Sprouting Seeds of Joy in the Manure of Life (Barbara Johnson)

The Art of Caregiving: How to Lend Support & Encouragement to Those with Cancer (Michael Barry)

What Cancer Cannot Do (Inspirio)

What Cancer Cannot Do: Stories of Courage (Phyllis Ten Elshof and Sarah M. Hupp)

When God and Cancer Meet: True Stories of Hope and Healing (Lynn Eib)

When Someone You Love Has Cancer: Comfort and Encouragement for Caregivers and Loved Ones (Cecil Murphey and Michal Sparks)

Caregiving / Hospice

A Caregiver's Survival Guide: How to Stay Healthy When Your Loved One Is Sick (Kay Marshall Strom)

Bedside Manners: A Practical Guide to Visiting the Ill (Katie Maxwell)

Called to Care: A Christian Worldview for Nursing (Judith Allen Shelly and Arlene B. Miller)

Caring for Aging Parents: Straight Answers That Help You Serve Their Needs Without Ignoring Your Own (Richard Johnson)

Loving Your Parents When They Can No Longer Love You (Terry D. Hargrave)

Not Alone: Encouragement for Caregivers (Nell E. Noonan)

The Art of Caregiving: How to Lend Support & Encouragement to Those with Cancer (Michael Barry)

Church Life, General

Baptism: The Believer's First Obedience (Larry E. Dyer)

In Remembrance of Me: A Manual on Observing the Lord's Supper (Jim Henry)

They Like Jesus But Not the Church: Insights from Emerging Generations (Dan Kimball)

Understanding Four Views on Baptism (Tom J. Nettles, Richard L. Pratt, Jr. and John H. Armstrong)

Church Life, Conflict / Dissension

Breaking the Bondage of Legalism: When Trying Harder Isn't Enough (Neil T. Anderson, Rich Miller and Paul Travis)

Facing Messy Stuff in the Church: Case Studies for Pastors and Congregations (Kenneth L. Swetland)

Firestorm: Preventing and Overcoming Church Conflicts (Ron Susek and D. James Kennedy)

The Wounded Minister: Healing from and Preventing Personal Attacks (Guy Greenfield and Brooks Faulkner)

Church Life, Emergent

Becoming Conversant with the Emerging Church: Understanding a Movement and Its Implications (D. A. Carson)

The Emerging Church: Vintage Christianity for New Generations (Dan A. Kimball, Renee N. Altson and Ivy Beckwith)

They Like Jesus But Not the Church: Insights from Emerging Generations (Dan Kimball)

Church Life, Small Groups

Discipleship Journal's Best Small-Group Ideas, Volume 1 (Discipleship Journal and The Navigators)

Group's Emergency Response Handbook: For Small Group Leaders (Roxanne Wieman)

How to Lead Small Groups (Neal F. McBride and Melody Carlson)

Leading Life-Changing Small Groups (Bill Donahue)

Making Small Groups Work: What Every Small Group Leader Needs to Know (Henry Cloud and John Sims Townsend)

Simple Small Groups: A User-Friendly Guide for Small Group Leaders (Bill Search)

Small Group Idea Book: Resources to Enrich Community, Worship, Prayer, Study, Outreach (Cindy Bunch)

Small Group Leadership as Spiritual Direction: Practical Ways to Blend an Ancient Art Into Your Contemporary Community (Heather Webb and Eugene H. Peterson)

Small Group Ministry in the 21st Century (M. Scott Boren)

Small Group Strategies: Ideas& Activities for Developing Spiritual Growth in Your Students (Charley Scandlyn and Laurie Polich)

The Big Book on Small Groups (Jeffrey Arnold)

The Search to Belong: Rethinking Intimacy, Community, and Small Groups (Joseph R. Myers, Renee N. Altson and Ivy Beckwith)

The Seven Deadly Sins of Small Group Ministry: A Troubleshooting Guide for Church Leaders (Bill Donahue and Russ Robinson)

Cloning / Biotech

Basic Questions on Genetics, Stem Cell Research, and Cloning: Are These Technologies Okay to Use? (Gary P. Stewart and John F. Kilner)

Human Dignity in the Biotech Century: A Christian Vision for Public Policy (Charles W. Colson and Nigel M. De S. Cameron)

Conflict

Can't Live with 'Em, Can't Live Without 'em: Dealing with the Love/Hate Relationships in Your Life (Stephen Arterburn and David A. Stoop)

Connecting: Healing Ourselves and Our Relationships (Larry Crabb)

Everybody's Normal Till You Get to Know Them (John Ortberg)

Men's Relational Toolbox (Gary Smalley and Greg Smalley and Michael Smalley)

Regret-Free Living: Hope for Past Mistakes and Freedom from Unhealthy Patterns (Stephen Arterburn and John Shore)

Relationships That Work: (And Those That Don't) (H. Norman Wright)

Safe People: How to Find Relationships That Are Good for You and Avoid Those That Aren't (Henry Cloud and John Sims Townsend)

Telling Each Other the Truth (William Backus)

The Five Languages of Apology: How to Experience Healing in All Your Relationships (Jennifer Thomas and Gary Chapman)

Who's Pushing Your Buttons? (John Townsend)

Why You Do the Things You Do: The Secret to Healthy Relationships (Timothy Clinton and Gary Sibcy)

Counseling

A Biblical Guide to Counseling the Sexual Addict (Steve Gallagher)

Competent Christian Counseling, Volume One: Foundations and Practice of Compassionate Soul Care (Timothy Clinton and George Ohlschlager)

Competent to Counsel: Introduction to Nouthetic Counseling (Jay Adams and Michael Smith)

Connecting: Healing Ourselves and Our Relationships (Larry Crabb)

Effective Marriage Counseling: The His Needs, Her Needs Guide to Helping Couples (Willard F., Jr. Harley)

Helping Those Who Hurt: A Handbook for Caring and Crisis (Barbara M. Roberts)

Helps for Counselors: A Mini-Manual for Christian Counseling (Jay Edward Adams)

Hope When You're Hurting: Answers to Four Questions Hurting People Ask (Larry Crabb and Dan B. Allender)

Hope-Focused Marriage Counseling: A Guide to Brief Therapy (Everett L. Worthington, Jr.)

Ministering to the Mourning: A Practical Guide for Pastors, Church Leaders, and Other Caregivers (Warren W. Wiersbe and David W. Wiersbe)

Quick Scripture Reference for Counseling (John G. Kruis)

Quick Scripture Reference for Counseling Women (Patricia A. Miller)

The Christian Counselor's Manual: The Practice of Nouthetic Counseling (Jay Edward Adams)

The Quick-Reference Guide to Biblical Counseling: Personal and Emotional Issues (Tim Clinton and Ron Hawkins)

The Quick-Reference Guide to Counseling Teenagers (Timothy E. Clinton and Chap Clark and Joshua Straub)

The Quick-Reference Guide to Marriage & Family Counseling (Tim Clinton and John Trent)

The Quick-Reference Guide to Sexuality & Relationship Counseling (Tim Clinton and Mark Laaser)

Culture / Postmodernism

Culture Making: Recovering Our Creative Calling (Andy Crouch)

Escape from Reason: A Penetrating Analysis of Trends in Modern Thought (Francis A. Schaeffer and J. P. Moreland)

How Now Shall We Live? (Charles W. Colson and Nancy Pearcey)

Dating / Singleness

Avoiding Mr. Wrong (and What to Do If You Didn't): Ten Men Who Will Ruin Your Life (Stephen Arterburn and Meg J. Rinck)

B4UD8: 7 Things You Need to Know Before Your Next Date (Hayley DiMarco and Michael DiMarco)

Boundaries in Dating: How Healthy Choices Grow Healthy Relationships (Henry Cloud and John Townsend)

Boy Meets Girl (Joshua Harris)

Breaking Up: He's Just Not That Into God (Stina Wilson)

Dateable: Are You? Are They? (Justin Lookadoo and Hayley Morgan)

Define the Relationship: A Candid Look at Breaking Up, Making Up, and Dating Well (Jeramy Clark and Jerusha Clark)

Falling in Love for All the Right Reasons: How to Find Your Soul Mate (Neil Clark Warren and Ken Abraham)

Finding Mr. Right: And How to Know When You Have (Stephen Arterburn and Meg J. Rinck)

Going Out Without Freaking Out: Dating Made Doable (Tim Baker)

He's Hot, She's Hot (Jeramy Clark and Jerusha Clark)

How to Get a Date Worth Keeping: Be Dating in Six Months or Your Money Back (Henry Cloud)

I Kissed Dating Goodbye: A New Attitude Toward Relationships and Romance (Joshua Harris)

If Singleness Is a Gift, What's the Return Policy? (Holly Virden and Michelle McKinney Hammond)

Is This the One?: Insightful Dates for Finding the Love of Your Life (Stephen Arterburn)

Lady in Waiting: Becoming God's Best While Waiting for Mr. Right (Jackie Kendall and Debby Jones)

Living Together: A Guide to Counseling Unmarried Couples (Jeff Vangoethem)

No-Nonsense Dating: Maximize Your Confidence and Recognize Your God-Given Soul Mate (Ronn Elmore)

Now and Not Yet: Making Sense of Single Life in the Twenty-First Century (Jennifer Marshall)

The Dateable Rules: A Guide to the Sexes (Justin Lookadoo and Hayley Morgan)

The Dirt on Dating (Hayley DiMarco)

The Five Love Languages Singles Edition (Gary Chapman)
The New Lady in Waiting: Becoming God's Best While Waiting for Mr. Right (Jackie Kendall and Debby Jones)
The Ten Commandments of Dating: Student Edition (Samuel Adams and Ben Young)
Things I Wish I'd Known Before We Got Married (Gary Chapman)
What to Do Until Love Finds You (Michelle McKinney Hammond)
What Women Wish You Knew about Dating: A Single Guy's Guide to Romantic Relationships (Stephen W. Simpson)

Depression

Blue Genes: Breaking Free from the Chemical Imbalances That Affect Your Moods, Your Mind, Your Life, and Your Loved Ones (Paul D. Meier and Todd Clements and Jean-Luc Bertrand)
Breaking Through Depression: A Biblical and Medical Approach to Emotional Wholeness (Donald P. Hall)
Broken Minds: Hope for Healing When You Feel Like You're "Losing It" (Steve Bloem and Robyn Bloem)
How to Win Over Depression (Tim LaHaye and Beverly LaHaye)
New Light on Depression: Help, Hope, and Answers for the Depressed and Those Who Love Them (David B. Biebel and Harold George Koenig)
Overcoming Anxiety and Depression: Practical Tools to Help You Deal with Negative Emotions (Bob Phillips)
Overcoming Depression: The Victory Over the Darkness Series (Neil T. Anderson and Joanne Anderson)
The Freedom from Depression Workbook (Les Carter and Frank B. Minirth)
Unmasking Male Depression (Archibald D. Hart)
Will Medicine Stop the Pain?: Finding God's Healing for Depression, Anxiety, & Other Troubling Emotions (Elyse Fitzpatrick and Laura Hendrickson)

Divorce / Remarriage

101 Questions to Ask Before You Get Remarried (H. Norman Wright)
A Woman's Guide to Healing the Heartbreak of Divorce (Rose Sweet)
Divorce and Remarriage in the Church: Biblical Solutions for Pastoral Realities (David Instone-Brewer)

Divorce Care: Hope, Help, and Healing During and After Your Divorce (Steve Grissom, Kathy Leonard and Timothy Smith)

Finding the Right One After Divorce: Avoiding the 13 Common Mistakes People Make in Remarriage (Edward M. Tauber and Jim Smoke)

From We to Me: Embracing Life Again After the Death or Divorce of a Spouse (Susan Zonnebelt-Smeenge and Robert DeVries)

Growing Through Divorce (Jim Smoke)

I Don't Want a Divorce: A 90 Day Guide to Saving Your Marriage (David Clarke and William G. Clarke)

Marriage, Divorce, and Remarriage in the Bible: A Fresh Look at What Scripture Teaches (Jay Edward Adams)

Moving Forward After Divorce: Practical Steps to Healing Your Hurts, Finding Fresh Perspective, Managing Your New Life (David Frisbie and Lisa Frisbie)

Moving Forward: A Devotional Guide for Finding Hope and Peace in the Midst of Divorce (Jim Smoke)

New Life After Divorce: The Promise of Hope Beyond the Pain (Bill Butterworth)

Reconcilable Differences: Defending Absolute Truth in a Relativistic World (Virginia Todd Holeman)

Remarriage After Divorce in Today's Church: 3 Views (Gordon J. Wenham, William A. Heth and Craig S. Keener)

The Complete Divorce Recovery Handbook (John P. Splinter and Margaret Rinck)

When He Leaves (Kari West and Noelle Quinn)

Divorce / Remarriage, Blended Families

Blended Families: Creating Harmony as You Build a New Home Life (Maxine Marsolini)

Living in a Step-Family Without Getting Stepped on: Helping Your Children Survive the Birth Order Blender (Kevin Leman)

The Smart Stepfamily: New Seven Steps to a Healthy Family (Ron L. Deal)

The Smart Stepmom: Practical Steps to Help You Thrive! (Ron L. Deal and Laura Petherbridge)

Divorce / Remarriage, Children of Divorce

Helping Children Survive Divorce (Archibald D. Hart)
Project 911: Divorce of Parents (Josh McDowell and Ed Stewart)
The Children of Divorce: The Loss of Family as the Loss of Being (Andrew Root)
What Children Need to Know When Parents Get Divorced (William L. Coleman)

Divorce / Remarriage, Separation

Broken Heart on Hold: Surviving Separation (Linda Rooks)
Hope for the Separated: Wounded Marriages Can Be Healed (Gary Chapman)

Doubt

Benefit of the Doubt: Breaking the Idol of Certainty (Gregory A. Boyd)
Clear Winter Nights: A Journey Into Truth, Doubt, and What Comes After (Trevin Wax)
Disappointment with God: Three Questions No One Asks Aloud (Philip Yancey)
Faith and Other Flat Tires: Searching for God on the Rough Road of Doubt (Andrea Palpant Dilley)

Eating Disorders

Diary of an Anorexic Girl (Morgan Menzie)
Empty: A Story of Anorexia (Christie Pettit)
Hope, Help, and Healing for Eating Disorders: A Whole-Person Approach to Treatment of Anorexia, Bulimia, and Disordered Eating (Gregory Jantz and Ann McMurray)
Love to Eat, Hate to Eat (Elyse Fitzpatrick)
The Monster Within: Facing an Eating Disorder (Cynthia Rowland McClure)
Thin Enough: My Spiritual Journey Through the Living Death of an Eating Disorder (Sheryle Cruse)

Environment / Global Warming / Simple Living

Gardening Eden: How Creation Care Will Change Your Faith, Your Life, and Our World (Michael Abbate and Randy Alcorn)

More or Less: Choosing a Lifestyle of Excessive Generosity (Jeff Shinabarger and Bob Goff)

Serve God, Save the Planet: A Christian Call to Action (J. Matthew Sleeth and Richard Cizik)

The Global-Warming Deception: How a Secret Elite Plans to Bankrupt America and Steal Your Freedom (Grant R. Jeffrey)

Evangelism

101 Ways to Reach Your Community (Steve Sjogren)

Becoming a Contagious Christian (Bill Hybels and Mark Mittelberg)

Conversational Evangelism: How to Listen and Speak So You Can Be Heard (Norman L. Geisler and David Geisler)

Emerging Hope: A Strategy for Reaching Postmodern Generations (Jimmy Long)

Evangelism and the Sovereignty of God (J. I. Packer and Mark Dever)

Evangelism Explosion 4th Edition (D. James Kennedy)

Evangelism for the Rest of Us: Sharing Christ Within Your Personality Style (Mike Bechtle)

Evangelism Outside the Box: New Ways to Help People Experience the Good News (Rick Richardson)

Finding Common Ground: How to Communicate with Those Outside the Christian Community . . . While We Still Can (Tim Downs)

Going Public with Your Faith: Becoming a Spiritual Influence at Work (William C. Peel and Walt Larimore)

Growing Your Faith by Giving It Away: Telling the Gospel Story with Grace and Passion (R. York Moore)

How to Lead a Seeker Bible Discussion: Discovering the Bible for Yourself (Rebecca Manley Pippert)

How to Share Your Faith (Greg Laurie)

I Love Mormons: A New Way to Share Christ with Latter-Day Saints (David L. Rowe)

Inside the Mind of Unchurched Harry and Mary: How to Reach Friends and Family Who Avoid God and the Church (Lee Strobel and Bill Hybels)

Just Walk Across the Room: Simple Steps Pointing People to Faith (Bill Hybels)

Looking at the Life of Jesus: 7 Seeker Bible Discussions on the Gospel of John (Rebecca Manley Pippert)

Out of the Saltshaker & Into the World: Evangelism as a Way of Life (Rebecca Manley Pippert)

Reaching the World in Our Own Backyard: A Guide to Building Relationships with People of Other Faiths and Cultures (Rajendra Pillai)

Sharing Your Faith with a Buddhist (Madasamy Thirumalai)

Sharing Your Faith with a Hindu (Madasamy Thirumalai)

Talking about Jesus Without Sounding Religious (Rebecca Manley Pippert)

The Complete Evangelism Guidebook: Expert Advice on Reaching Others for Christ (Scott Dawson and Luis Palau)

The Master Plan of Evangelism (Robert E. Coleman)

The Reason for God: Belief in an Age of Skepticism (Timothy Keller)

Way of Jesus (Rebecca Manley Pippert)

Fasting

7 Basic Steps to Successful Fasting & Prayer (Bill Bright)

A Hunger for God: Desiring God Through Fasting and Prayer (John Piper, David Platt and Francis Chan)

Fasting for Spiritual Breakthrough: A Guide to Nine Biblical Fasts (Elmer L. Towns)

Tony Evans Speaks Out on Fasting (Tony Evans)

Forgiveness / Reconciliation

Am I Forgiving? (Jeannie St. John Taylor)

Art of Forgiving (Lewis B. Smedes)

Authentic Relationships: Discover the Lost Art of "One Anothering" (Wayne Jacobsen and Clay Jacobsen)

Choosing Forgiveness: Your Journey to Freedom (Nancy Leigh DeMoss and Lawrence Kimbrough)

Choosing to Forgive Workbook (Les Carter and Frank B. Minirth)

Do Yourself a Favor . . . Forgive: Learn How to Take Control of Your Life Through Forgiveness (Joyce Meyer)

Forgive and Forget: Healing the Hurts We Don't Deserve (Lewis B. Smedes)

Forgiveness (Matthew West)

Forgiveness: Finding Peace Through Letting Go (Adam Hamilton)

Forgiving and Reconciling: Finding Our Way Through Cultural Challenges (Everett L. Worthington, Jr.)

One Light Still Shines: My Life Beyond the Shadow of the Amish School-house Shooting (Marie Monville and Cindy Lambert)

The Forgiveness Project: The Startling Discovery of How to Overcome Cancer, Find Health, and Achieve Peace (Michael S. Barry)

The Freedom and Power of Forgiveness (John MacArthur)

The Gift of Forgiveness (Charles F. Stanley)

When You've Been Wronged: Overcoming Barriers to Reconciliation (Erwin W. Lutzer)

You Wouldn't Love Me If You Knew (Jeannie St. John Taylor)

Friendship

Authentic Relationships: Discover the Lost Art of "One Anothering" (Wayne Jacobsen and Clay Jacobsen)

The Friendship Factor: How to Get Closer to the People You Care for (Alan Loy McGinnis)

The Friendships of Women: The Beauty and Power of God's Plan for Us (Dee Brestin and Priscilla Evans Shirer)

God's Will / Purpose

Chasing Daylight: Dare to Live a Life of Adventure (Erwin Raphael McManus)

Cure for the Common Life (Max Lucado)

Decision Making and the Will of God (Garry Friesen and J. Robin Maxson)

Discovering God's Will: How to Know When You Are Heading in the Right Direction (Andy Stanley and Reggie Joiner)

Don't Waste Your Life (John Piper)

Experiencing God: Knowing and Doing the Will of God (Henry Blackaby, Richard Blackaby and Claude King)

Listening to God in Times of Choice: Living Between How It Is & How It Ought to Be (Gordon T. Smith)

Living the Life God Has Planned: A Guide to Knowing God's Will (Bill Thrasher and Joseph M. Stowell)

The Call: Finding and Fulfilling the Central Purpose of Your Life (Os Guinness)

The Purpose Driven Life: What on Earth Am I Here For? (Rick Warren)

Grief

Grief, Death of a Child

I'll Hold You in Heaven: Healing and Hope for the Parent Who Has Lost a Child Through Miscarriage, Stillbirth, Abortion or Early Infant Death (Jack W. Hayford)

Mommy, Please Don't Cry: There Are No Tears in Heaven (Linda Deymaz and Laurie Snow Hein)

Not by Accident (Isabel Fleece)

Safe in the Arms of God: Truth from Heaven about the Death of a Child (John F. MacArthur, Jr. and Stephen M. Miller)

Surviving the Loss of a Child: Support for Grieving Parents (Elizabeth B. Brown)

Without a Word: How a Boy's Unspoken Love Changed Everything (Jill Kelly and Tim McGraw and Faith Hill)

Grief, Death of a Parent

When Your Father Dies: How a Man Deals with the Loss of His Father (Dave Veerman and Bruce Barton)

Grief, Death of a Spouse

Getting to the Other Side of Grief: Overcoming the Loss of a Spouse (Susan J. Zonnebelt-Smeenge and Robert C. de Vries)

Learning to Breathe Again: Choosing Life and Finding Hope After a Shattering Loss (Tammy Trent)

Let Me Grieve, But Not Forever: A Journey Out of the Darkness of Loss (Verdell Davis)

The Tender Scar: Life After the Death of a Spouse (Richard Mabry)

Grief, Helping Children Grieve

Children and Grief: Helping Your Child Understand Death (Joey O'Connor)

Helping Children Grieve: When Someone They Love Dies (Theresa M. Huntley)

If Nathan Were Here (Mary Bahr and Karen A. Jerome)

It's Okay to Cry: A Parent's Guide to Helping Children Through the Losses of Life (H. Norman Wright)

Someday Heaven (Larry Libby and Wayne McLoughlin)

Someone I Love Died (Christine Harder Tangvald and Anne Kennedy)

Water Bugs and Dragonflies: Explaining Death to Children (Doris Stickney)
What Happens When We Die? (Carolyn Nystrom, Wayne A. Hanna and Eira Reeves)

Heaven / Hell

55 Answers to Questions about Life After Death (Mark Hitchcock)
Erasing Hell: What God Said about Eternity, and the Things We Made Up (Francis Chan and Preston Sprinkle)
Four Views on Hell (John Walvoord and Zachary J. Hayes and William Crockett)
Heaven (Randy Alcorn)
Heaven Is for Real: A Little Boy's Astounding Story of His Trip to Heaven and Back (Todd Burpo and Lynn Vincent)
Heaven: My Father's House (Anne Graham Lotz)
Heaven: Your Real Home (Joni Eareckson Tada)
The Glory of Heaven: The Truth about Heaven, Angels, and Eternal Life (John MacArthur)
Tony Evans Speaks Out on Heaven and Hell (Tony Evans)
Your Eternal Reward: Triumph and Tears at the Judgment Seat of Christ (Erwin W. Lutzer)

Heaven / Hell, Children

Heaven Is for Real for Kids (Todd Burpo, Sonja Burpo and Colton Burpo)
Heaven Is for Real for Little Ones (Todd Burpo and Sonja Burpo)
Someone I Love Died (Christine Harder Tangvald and Anne Kennedy)
What about Heaven? (Kathleen Bostrom and Elena Kucharik)
What Happened When Grandma Died (Peggy Barker and Patricia Mattozzi)
What Is Heaven Like? (Beverly Lewis and Pam Querin)

Holidays / Traditions

Celebrations That Touch the Heart: Creative Ideas to Make Your Holidays and Special Events Meaningful (Brenda Poinsett)
If You're Missing Baby Jesus: A True Story That Embraces the Spirit of Christmas (Jean Jeffrey Gietzen and Lila Rose Kennedy)

The Case for Christmas: A Journalist Investigates the Identity of the Child in the Manger (Lee Strobel)

The Case for the Resurrection of Jesus (Gary R. Habermas and Michael R. Licona)

Holidays / Traditions, Children

Benjamin's Box: The Story of the Resurrection Eggs (Melody Carlson, Jack Stockman and Barbara Rainey)

Clopper the Christmas Donkey (Emily King and Ed Olson)

Shaoey and Dot: A Christmas Miracle (Mary Beth Chapman, Steven Curtis Chapman and Jim Chapman)

Squanto and the Miracle of Thanksgiving (Eric Metaxas and Shannon Stirnweis)

The Legend of the Candy Cane: The Inspirational Story of Our Favorite Christmas Candy (Lori Walburg and Richard Cowdrey)

The Tale of Three Trees: A Traditional Folktale (Angela Elwell Hunt and Tim Jonke)

Homosexuality

101 Frequently Asked Questions about Homosexuality (Mike Haley)

Called Out: A Former Lesbian's Discovery of Freedom (Janet Boynes)

Can Homosexuality Be Healed? (Francis Macnutt)

Coming Out of Homosexuality: New Freedom for Men and Women (Bob Davies and Lori Rentzel)

Desires in Conflict (Joe Dallas)

God's Grace and the Homosexual Next Door: Reaching the Heart of the Gay Men and Women in Your World (Alan Chambers)

Homosexuality and the Christian: A Guide for Parents, Pastors, and Friends (Mark A. Yarhouse)

Into the Promised Land: Beyond the Lesbian Struggle (Jeanette Howard)

Leaving Homosexuality (Alan Chambers)

Parent's Guide to Preventing Homosexuality (Joseph Nicolosi and Linda Ames Nicolosi)

Restoring Sexual Identity (Anne Paulk)

Same-Sex Partnerships? A Christian Perspective (John R. W. Stott)

Someone I Love Is Gay: How Family & Friends Can Respond (Bob Davies and Anita Worthen)

The Complete Christian Guide to Understanding Homosexuality (Joe Dallas and Nancy Heche)

The Gay Agenda: It's Dividing the Family, the Church and a Nation (Ronnie W. Floyd)

The Gay Gospel? How Pro-Gay Advocates Misread the Bible (Joe Dallas)

The Homosexual Agenda: Exposing the Principal Threat to Religious Freedom Today (Alan Sears and Craig Osten)

The Same Sex Controversy: Defending and Clarifying the Bible's Message about Homosexuality (James White and Jeffrey D. Niell)

What Do I Say to a Friend Who's Gay? (Emily Parke Chase)

What's Wrong with Same-Sex Marriage? (D. James Kennedy and Jerry Newcombe)

When Homosexuality Hits Home: What to Do When a Loved One Says They're Gay (Joe Dallas)

Hopelessness / Brokenness / Bondage

Boundaries: When to Say Yes, How to Say No, to Take Control of Your Life (Henry Cloud and John Townsend)

Bridge Called Hope: Stories of Triumph from the Ranch of Rescued Dreams (Kim Meeder)

Changes That Heal: The Four Shifts That Make Everything Better and That Anyone Can Do (Henry Cloud)

Deadly Emotions: Understand the Mind-Body-Spirit Connection That Can Heal or Destroy You (Don Colbert)

Healing for Damaged Emotions (David A. Seamands and Gary R. Collins)

Hope Rising (Kim Meeder)

Letting God Meet Your Emotional Needs (Cindi McMenamin)

Released from Bondage (Neil Anderson and Fernando Garzon and Judy King)

The Bondage Breaker (Neil T. Anderson)

The Cure for the Chronic Life: Overcoming the Hopelessness That Holds You Back (Deanna Favre, Shane Stanford and Max Lucado)

The Wounded Warrior: A Survival Guide for When You're Beat Up, Burned Out, or Battle Weary (Steve Stephens)

When Your Past Is Hurting Your Present (Sue Augustine)

Wounds That Heal: Bringing Our Hurts to the Cross (Stephen A. Seamands)

Your Scars Are Beautiful to God: Finding Peace and Purpose in the Hurts of Your Past (Sharon Jaynes)

Hospital

When Your Doctor Has Bad News: Simple Steps to Strength, Healing, and Hope (Al B. Weir and Joni Eareckson Tada)

Infertility

Empty Womb, Aching Heart: Hope and Help for Those Struggling with Infertility (Marlo M. Schalesky)

The Infertility Companion: Hope and Help for Couples Facing Infertility (Sandra L. Glahn and William R. Cutrer)

When You Are Coping with Infertility (Vera Snow)

Leadership

Biblical Eldership (Alexander Strauch)

Called to Be God's Leader: How God Prepares His Servants for Spiritual Leadership (Henry T. Blackaby and Richard Blackaby)

Developing the Leader Within You (John C. Maxwell)

Elders and Leaders: God's Plan for Leading the Church: A Biblical, Historical and Cultural Perspective (Gene A. Getz and Brad Smith and Bob Buford)

In the Name of Jesus: Reflections on Christian Leadership (Henri J. M. Nouwen)

Jesus on Leadership: Timeless Wisdom on Servant Leadership (C. Gene Wilkes and Win Mumma)

Leading with a Limp: Take Full Advantage of Your Most Powerful Weakness (Dan B. Allender)

Next Generation Leader: Five Essentials for Those Who Will Shape the Future (Andy Stanley)

Preventing Ministry Failure: A ShepherdCare Guide for Pastors, Ministers and Other Caregivers (Michael Todd Wilson, Brad Hoffmann and Members of Caregivers Forum)

Spiritual Leadership: Principles of Excellence for Every Believer (J. Oswald Sanders)

The Book on Leadership (John MacArthur)

Manners / Virtue / Character

A Little Book of Manners for Boys (Bob Barnes, Michal Sparks and Emilie Barnes)

A Little Book of Manners: Courtesy & Kindness for Young Ladies (Emilie Barnes, Anne C. Buchanan and Michal Sparks)

As Iron Sharpens Iron: Building Character in a Mentoring Relationship (Howard Hendricks and Williams Hendricks)

Child's Book of Character Building, Book 1: Growing Up in God's World- At Home, at School, at Play (Ron Coriell and Rebekah Coriell)

The Book of Virtues: A Treasury of Great Moral Stories (William J. Bennett)

The Children's Book of Virtues (William J. Bennett and Michael Hague)

Marriage

Boundaries in Marriage (Henry Cloud and John Sims Townsend)

Choosing God's Best: Wisdom for Lifelong Romance (Don Raunikar)

For Couples Only: Eye-opening Insights about How the Opposite Sex Thinks: Contains the Best Sellers "For Women Only" and "For Men Only" (Shaunti Feldhahn and Jeff Feldhahn)

From Anger to Intimacy: How Forgiveness Can Transform Your Marriage (Gary Smalley and Ted Cunningham)

Great Parents, Lousy Lovers: Discover How to Enjoy Life with Your Spouse While Raising Your Kids (Gary Smalley and Ted Cunningham)

Healing the Hurt in Your Marriage (Gray Rosberg and Barbara Rosberg)

Healing Your Marriage When Trust Is Broken (Cindy Beall and Craig Groeschel)

Hedges: Loving Your Marriage Enough to Protect It [With DVD] (Jerry B. Jenkins and Tim LaHaye)

I, Isaac, Take Thee, Rebekah: Moving from Romance to Lasting Love (Ravi Zacharias)

Love as a Way of Life: Seven Keys to Transforming Every Aspect of Your Life (Gary Chapman)

Love Busters: Protecting Your Marriage from Habits That Destroy Romantic Love (Willard F. Harley, Jr.)

The 5 Love Needs of Men and Women (Gary Rosberg and Barbara Rosberg)

When I Get Married: Surrendering the Fantasy, Embracing the Reality (Jerusha Clark)

Marriage, Adultery

Close Calls: What Adulterers Want You to Know about Protecting Your Marriage (Dave Carder, M.A.)

His Needs, Her Needs: Building an Affair-Proof Marriage (Willard F. Harley, Jr.)

Shattered Vows: Hope and Healing for Women Who Have Been Sexually Betrayed (Debra Laaser)

Surviving an Affair (Willard F. Harley, Jr. and Jennifer Harley Chalmers)

The Healing Choice: How to Move Beyond Betrayal (Brenda Stoeker and Susan Allen)

Torn Asunder: Recovering from an Extramarital Affair (Dave Carder, M.A., Duncan Jaenicke and John Townsend)

Marriage, For Women

7 Things He'll Never Tell You: But You Need to Know (Kevin Leman)

Have a New Husband by Friday: How to Change His Attitude, Behavior & Communication in 5 Days (Kevin Leman)

Why Can't He Be More Like Me? 9 Secrets to Understanding Your Husband (Poppy Smith)

Marriage, Newlyweds

A Celebration of Sex for Newlyweds (Douglas E. Rosenau)

Getting Your Sex Life Off to a Great Start (Clifford L. Penner and Joyce J. Penner)

Marriage, Nonbelieving Spouse

Beloved Unbeliever: Loving Your Husband Into the Faith (Jo Berry and Heather Berry)

Can Two Walk Together?: Encouragement for Spiritually Unbalanced Marriages (Sabrina D. Black, Gary Collins and Ed Hindson)

Surviving a Spiritual Mismatch in Marriage (Lee Strobel and Leslie Strobel)

When He Doesn't Believe: Help and Encouragement for Women Who Feel Alone in Their Faith (Nancy Kennedy)

Marriage, Pornography Within Marriage

Every Heart Restored: A Wife's Guide to Healing in the Wake of a Husband's Sexual Sin (Fred Stoeker and Brenda Stoeker and Mike Yorkey)

Living with Your Husband's Secret Wars (Marsha Means)
When His Secret Sin Breaks Your Heart: Letters to Hurting Wives (Kathy Gallagher and Beverly LaHaye)

Marriage, Sexual Issues

A Celebration of Sex After 50 (Douglas E. Rosenau, James Childerston and Carolyn Childers)
Intimate Issues: Twenty-One Questions Christian Women Ask about Sex (Linda Dillow and Lorraine Pintus)
Love, Sex, and Lasting Relationships (Chip Ingram)
Sacred Sex: A Spiritual Celebration of Oneness in Marriage (Tim Alan Gardner and Scott M. Stanley)
Sex Begins in the Kitchen: Creating Intimacy to Make Your Marriage Sizzle (Kevin Leman)
Sheet Music SC (Repkg): Uncovering the Secrets of Sexual Intimacy in Marriage (Kevin Leman)
The Act of Marriage: The Beauty of Sexual Love (Tim LaHaye and Beverly LaHaye)
The Gift of Sex: A Guide to Sexual Fulfillment (Clifford L. Penner and Joyce Penner)
Under the Sheets: The Secrets to Hot Sex in Your Marriage (Kevin Leman)
When Two Become One: Enhancing Sexual Intimacy in Marriage (Christopher McCluskey and Rachel McCluskey)

Menopause / Hormones

When Your Hormones Go Haywire: Solutions for Women Over 40 (Pamela M. Smith)

Men's Issues

At the Altar of Sexual Idolatry (Steve Gallagher)
Every Man, God's Man: Courageous Faith and Daily Integrity (Stephen Arterburn)
Every Man's Challenge: How Far Are You Willing to Go for God? (Stephen Arterburn, Fred Stoeker and Mike Yorkey)
Every Single Man's Battle: Staying on the Path of Sexual Purity (Stephen Arterburn and Fred Stoeker)
Fight: Are You Willing to Pick a Fight with Evil? (Kenny Luck)

For Men Only: A Straightforward Guide to the Inner Lives of Women (Shaunti Feldhahn and Jeff Feldhahn)

God's Gift to Women (Eric Ludy)

King Me: What Every Son Wants and Needs from His Father (Steve Farrar)

Men's Secret Wars (Patrick Means)

No More Christian Nice Guy: When Being Nice—Instead of Good—Hurts Men, Women and Children (Paul Coughlin and Laura C. Schlessinger)

Pure Eyes: A Man's Guide to Sexual Integrity (Craig Gross and Steven Luff)

Road Warrior: How to Keep Your Faith, Relationships, and Integrity When Away from Home (Stephen Arterburn and Sam Gallucci)

Seven Seasons of the Man in the Mirror (Patrick Morley)

Sex and the Single Guy: Winning Your Battle for Purity (Joseph Knable)

Tactics: Securing the Victory in Every Young Man's Battle (Fred Stoeker and Mike Yorkey)

Temptations Men Face: Straightforward Talk on Power, Money, Affairs, Perfectionism, Insensitivity (Tom L. Eisenman)

The Game Plan (Joe Dallas)

The Man in the Mirror: Solving the 24 Problems Men Face (Patrick Morley)

When Good Men Are Tempted (Bill Perkins)

Wild at Heart: Discovering the Secret of a Man's Soul (John Eldredge)

Mental Illness

Darkness Is My Only Companion: A Christian Response to Mental Illness (Kathryn Greene-McCreight)

When Your Family Is Living with Mental Illness (Marcia Lund)

Mentoring / Discipleship

Mobilizing Men for One-On-One Ministry (Steve Sonderman)

The Cost of Discipleship (Dietrich Bonhoeffer)

The Young Man in the Mirror: A Rite of Passage Into Manhood (Patrick Morley)

Miracles

Miracles (C. S. Lewis)

Miscarriage

Empty Arms: Hope and Support for Those Who Have Suffered a Miscarriage, Stillbirth, or Tubal Pregnancy (Pamela W. Vredevelt and Arnold Petersen)

Free to Grieve: Healing and Encouragement for Those Who Have Suffered Miscarriage and Stillbirth (Maureen Rank)

Grieving the Child I Never Knew: A Devotional for Comfort in the Loss of Your Unborn or Newly Born Child (Kathe Wunnenberg)

Hannah's Hope: Seeking God's Heart in the Midst of Infertility, Miscarriage, and Adoption Loss (Jennifer Saake and Barbara Deane)

I'll Hold You in Heaven: Healing and Hope for the Parent Who Has Lost a Child Through Miscarriage, Stillbirth, Abortion or Early Infant Death (Jack W. Hayford)

Silent Grief: Miscarriage-Finding Your Way Through the Darkness (Clara Hinton)

When Your Baby Dies: Through Miscarriage or Stillbirth (Louis A. Gamino and Ann T. Cooney)

Missions

How to Get Ready for Short-Term Missions (Anne-Geri' Fann and Gregory Taylor)

Is That Really You, God? Hearing the Voice of God (Loren Cunningham)

Mack and Leeann's Guide to Short-Term Missions (J. Mack Stiles and Leeann Stiles)

Mission Trip Prep Kit Leader's Guide: Complete Preparation for Your Students' Cross-Cultural Experience (Kevin Johnson)

Operation World: The Definitive Prayer Guide to Every Nation (Jason Mandryk)

Peace Child: An Unforgettable Story of Primitive Jungle Treachery in the 20th Century (Don Richardson)

Short-Term Missions Workbook: From Mission Tourists to Global Citizens (Tim Dearborn)

When Helping Hurts: How to Alleviate Poverty Without Hurting the Poor . . . and Yourself (Steve Corbett, Brian Fikkert and David Platt)

Names of God

Lord, I Want to Know You: A Devotional Study on the Names of God (Kay Arthur)

Names of Christ (T. C. Horton, Charles Hurlburt and James Bell)
The Names of God (Kenneth S. Hemphill)

New Believers

Basic Christianity (John Stott and Rick Warren)
Basics for Believers: Foundational Truths to Guide Your Life (William L. Thrasher, Jr. and Alistair Begg)
Growing in Christ: A 13-Week Course for New and Growing Christians (The Navigators)
Knowing Jesus Christ, Book 1 (The Navigators)
Mere Christianity (C. S. Lewis)
New Christian's Handbook: Everything New Believers Need to Know (Max Anders)
Your Life in Christ (NavPress)

Other Religions

Jesus Among Other Gods: The Absolute Claims of the Christian Message (Ravi K. Zacharias)
So What's the Difference? A Look at 20 Worldviews, Faiths and Religions and How They Compare to Christianity (Fritz Ridenour)
The Kingdom of the Cults (Walter Ralston Martin and Ravi K. Zacharias)
Unspeakable: Facing Up to the Challenge of Evil (Os Guinness)

Parenting

21 Ways to Connect with Your Kids (Kathi Lipp and Cheri Gregory)
Boundaries with Kids: When to Say Yes, When to Say No to Help Your Children Gain Control of Their Lives (Henry Cloud and John Sims Townsend)
Building the Christian Family You Never Had: A Practical Guide for Pioneer Parents (Mary E. Demuth)
Cleaning House: A Mom's Twelve-Month Experiment to Rid Her Home of Youth Entitlement (Kay Wills Wyma and Michael Gurian)
Creative Correction: Extraordinary Ideas for Everyday Discipline (Lisa Whelchel)
Guarding Your Child's Heart: Establish Your Child's Faith Through Scripture Memory and Meditation (Gary Smalley)

Have a Happy Family by Friday: How to Improve Communication, Respect & Teamwork in 5 Days (Kevin Leman)

Have a New Kid by Friday: How to Change Your Child's Attitude, Behavior & Character in 5 Days (Kevin Leman)

How to Talk So Your Kids Will Listen: From Toddlers to Teenagers-Connecting with Your Children at Every Age (H. Norman Wright)

Parenting with Love and Logic: Teaching Children Responsibility (Foster Cline and Jim Fay)

Peacemaking for Families (Ken Sande and Tom Raabe)

Preparing Him for the Other Woman: A Mother's Guide to Raising Her Son to Love a Wife and Lead a Family (Sheri Rose Shepherd)

Rite of Passage Parenting: Four Essential Experiences to Equip Your Kids for Life (Walker Moore)

Shepherding a Child's Heart (Tedd Tripp and David Powlison)

The 5 Love Languages of Children (Gary Chapman and Ross Campbell)

The Love Dare for Parents (Stephen Kendrick, Alex Kendrick and Lawrence Kimbrough)

The New Dare to Discipline (James C. Dobson)

The New Strong-Willed Child: Birth Through Adolescence (James C. Dobson)

What Dads Need to Know about Daughters/What Moms Need to Know about Sons (John Burns and Helen Burns)

What Every Mom Needs (Elisa Morgan and Carol Kuykendall)

What He Must Be: If He Wants to Marry My Daughter (Voddie Baucham, Jr.)

When Your Child's Marriage Ends (Mildred Tengbom)

You Can't Make Me (But I Can Be Persuaded): Strategies for Bringing Out the Best in Your Strong-Willed Child (Cynthia Ulrich Tobias)

Parenting, Autism / Special Needs

An Unexpected Joy: The Gift of Parenting a Challenging Child (Mary Sharp and Eugene H. Peterson)

Autism's Hidden Blessings: Discovering God's Promises for Autistic Children & Their Families (Kelly Langston)

Dancing with Max: A Mother and Son Who Broke Free (Emily Colson and Charles Colson)

Empowering Your Child Who Has Special Needs (Debbie Salter Goodwin)

Facing Autism: Giving Parents Reasons for Hope and Guidance for Help (Lynn M. Hamilton and Bernard Rimland)

The ADHD-Autism Connection: A Step Toward More Accurate Diagnoses and Effective Treatments (Diane Kennedy)

Parenting, Boys

A Boy After God's Own Heart: Your Awesome Adventure with Jesus (Jim George)

Bringing Up Boys (James C. Dobson)

King Me: What Every Son Wants and Needs from His Father (Steve Farrar)

Raising a Modern-Day Joseph: A Timeless Strategy for Growing Great Kids (Larry Fowler)

Parenting, Empty Nest

Give Them Wings (Carol Kuykendall)

The Second Half of Marriage: Facing the Eight Challenges of the Empty-Nest Years [With Discussion Guide] (David Arp and Claudia Arp)

Parenting, Fathering

88 Great Daddy-Daughter Dates: Fun, Easy & Creative Ways to Build Memories Together (Rob Teigen and Joanna Teigen)

Anchor Man: How a Father Can Anchor His Family in Christ for the Next 100 Years (Steve Farrar)

Dad, If You Only Knew . . . (Josh Weidmann and Jim Weidmann)

Daddy Dates: Four Daughters, One Clueless Dad, and His Quest to Win Their Hearts (Greg Wright)

Daughters Gone Wild, Dads Gone Crazy: Battle-Tested Tips from a Father and Daughter Who Survived the Teenage Years (Charles Stone and Heather Stone)

Fathering Like the Father: Becoming the Dad God Wants You to Be (Kenneth O. Gangel and Jeffery S. Gangel and Howard G. Hendricks)

Raising a Modern Day Knight: A Father's Role in Guiding His Son to Authentic Manhood (Robert Lewis)

Rookie Dad: Thoughts on First-Time Fatherhood (David Jacobsen)

The Father Connection: How You Can Make the Difference in Your Child's Self-Esteem and Sense of Purpose (Josh McDowell)

What a Difference a Daddy Makes: The Lasting Imprint a Dad Leaves on His Daughter's Life (Kevin Leman)
What Happened to My Little Girl? Dad's Ultimate Guide to His Tween Daughter (Nancy Rue and Jim Rue)

Parenting, Girls

A Girl After God's Own Heart (Elizabeth George)
Bringing Up Girls: Practical Advice and Encouragement for Those Shaping the Next Generation of Women (James C. Dobson)

Parenting, Grandparenting

101 Ways to Love Your Grandkids: Sharing Your Life and God's Love (Bob Barnes and Emilie Barnes)
Generation G: Advice for Savvy Grandmothers Who Will Never Go Gray (Marty Norman)
Long Distance Grandma: Staying Connected Across the Miles (Janet Teitsort)
The Power of a Godly Grandparent: Leaving a Spiritual Legacy (Stephen A. Bly)

Parenting, Mothering

Beyond Bath Time: Embracing Motherhood as a Sacred Role (Erin Davis)
Life Interrupted: The Scoop on Being a Young Mom (Tricia Goyer)
Preparing Him for the Other Woman: A Mother's Guide to Raising Her Son to Love a Wife and Lead a Family (Sheri Rose Shepherd)
What a Difference a Mom Makes: The Indelible Imprint a Mom Leaves on Her Son's Life (Kevin Leman)

Parenting, New Baby

Before You Were Born (Nancy White Carlstrom and Linda Saport)
Getting to Know You: A Journal for Expecting Parents (Christine M. Dorn)
God Gave Us Two (Lisa Tawn Bergren and Laura J. Bryant)
The Best-Ever Christian Baby Name Book: Thousands of Names and Their Meanings (Nick Harrison and Steve Miller)
Your Marriage Can Survive a Newborn (Glenn Williams and Natalie Williams)

Parenting, New Moms

365 Things Every New Mom Should Know: A Daily Guide to Loving and Nurturing Your Child (Linda Danis)

First-Time Mom: Getting Off on the Right Foot from Birth to First Grade (Kevin Leman)

The New Mom's Guide to Life with Baby (Susan Besze Wallace and Monica Reed)

Parenting, Prodigal Children

Praying for Your Prodigal (Kyle Idleman)

Praying for Your Prodigal Daughter: Hope, Help & Encouragement for Hurting Parents (Janet Thompson)

Prodigals and Those Who Love Them: Words of Encouragement for Those Who Wait (Ruth Bell Graham)

The Hurting Parent: Help and Hope for Parents of Prodigals (Margie M. Lewis and Gregg Lewis)

Parenting, Sex Education

A Chicken's Guide to Talking Turkey with Your Kids about Sex (Kathy Flores Bell and Kevin Leman)

Before I Was Born (Carol Nystrom and Sandra Speidel)

Straight Talk with Your Kids about Sex (Josh McDowell and Dottie McDowell)

Teaching Your Children Healthy Sexuality: A Biblical Approach to Prepare Them for Life (Jim Burns)

The Ultimate Girls' Body Book: Not-So-Silly Questions about Your Body (Walt Larimore and Amaryllis Sanchez Wohlever)

The Ultimate Guys Body Book: Not-So-Stupid Questions about Your Body (Walt Larimore, MD and Guy Francis)

Parenting, Single Parenting

Financial Relief for Single Parents: A Proven Plan for Achieving the Seemingly Impossible (Brenda Armstrong)

God Loves Single Moms: Practical Help for Finding Confidence, Strength, and Hope (Teresa Whitehurst)

Single Parenting That Works: Six Keys to Raising Happy, Healthy Children in a Single-Parent Home (Kevin Leman)

Parenting, Stepparenting

Dating and the Single Parent (Ron L. Deal and Dennis Rainey)
The Smart Stepdad: Steps to Help You Succeed! (Ron L. Deal)
The Smart Stepfamily: 7 Steps to a Healthy Family (Ron L. Deal and Gary Chapman)
The Smart Stepfamily: New Seven Steps to a Healthy Family (Ron L. Deal)

Parenting, Teens / Adolescence

Boundaries with Teens: When to Say Yes, How to Say No (John Townsend)
Dear Mom: Everything Your Teenage Daughter Wants You to Know But Will Never Tell You (Melody Carlson)
Have a New Teenager by Friday: From Mouthy and Moody to Respectful and Responsible in 5 Days (Kevin Leman)
Hope for Parents of Troubled Teens: A Practical Guide to Getting Them Back on Track (Connie Rae)
I'm Pregnant, Now What? Heartfelt Advice on Getting Through an Unplanned Pregnancy (Ruth Graham and Sara Dormon, Ph.D)
Parenting Today's Adolescent: Helping Your Child Avoid the Traps of the Preteen and Teen Years (Dennis Rainey and Barbara Rainey and Bruce Nygren)
Preparing for Adolescence: How to Survive the Coming Years of Change (James C. Dobson)
Raising Responsible Teens in a Digital World (Brian Housman)
Stressed or Depressed: A Practical and Inspirational Guide for Parents of Hurting Teens (Archibald D. Hart and Catherine Hart Weber)
Teenage Boys: Surviving and Enjoying These Extraordinary Years (Bill Beausay)
The 5 Love Languages of Teenagers (Gary Chapman)
The Fight of Your Life: Why Your Teen Is at Risk & What Only You Can Do about It (Jeffrey Dean)
The Seven Cries of Today's Teens: Hear Their Hearts, Make the Connection (Tim Smith and George Gallup, Jr.)
Understanding Your Young Teen: Practical Wisdom for Parents (Mark Oestreicher)
What Your Daughter Isn't Telling You: Expert Insight Into the World of Teen Girls (Susie Shellenberger and Kathy Gowler)

When Kids Hurt: Help for Adults Navigating the Adolescent Maze (Chap Clark and Steve Rabey)
Why Christian Kids Rebel: Trading Heartache for Hope (Tim Kimmel)

Physical Disabilities

Lessons I Learned in the Light: All You Need to Thrive in a Dark World (Jennifer Rothschild)

Pornography/Sex Addiction

A Biblical Guide to Counseling the Sexual Addict (Steve Gallagher)
Breaking Free: Understanding Sexual Addiction & the Healing Power of Jesus (Russell Willingham and Bob Davies)
Every Heart Restored: A Wife's Guide to Healing in the Wake of a Husband's Sexual Sin (Fred Stoeker and Brenda Stoeker and Mike Yorkey)
Healing the Wounds of Sexual Addiction (Mark Laaser, Debra Laaser and Gary Smalley)
Hope After Betrayal: Healing When Sexual Addiction Invades Your Marriage (Meg Wilson)
I Surrender All: Rebuilding a Marriage Broken by Pornography (Clay Crosse, Renee Crosse and Mark Tabb)
My Husband Has a Secret: Finding Healing for the Betrayal of Sexual Addiction (Molly Ann Miller)
The Silent War: Ministering to Those Caught in the Deception of Pornography (Henry J. Rogers and Norm Miller)

Prayer

Fresh Wind, Fresh Fire: What Happens When God's Spirit Invades the Heart of His People (Jim Cymbala and Dean Merrill)
Intercessory Prayer: How God Can Use Your Prayers to Move Heaven and Earth (Dutch Sheets)
Power Through Prayer (Edward M. Bounds)
Prayer: Does It Make Any Difference? (Philip Yancey)
Praying the Names of God: A Daily Guide (Ann Spangler)
The Power of a Praying Parent (Stormie Omartian)
The Power of a Praying Wife Deluxe Edition (Stormie Omartian)
The Power of a Praying Woman (Stormie Omartian)
Too Busy Not to Pray: Slowing Down to Be with God (Bill Hybels)

Pregnancy

Expecting: Praying for Your Child's Development-Body and Soul (Marla Taviano)

Love Letters to My Baby: A Guided Journal for Expectant and New Mothers (Vickey Banks and Sophie Allport)

Surprise Child: Finding Hope in Unexpected Pregnancy (Leslie Leyland Fields)

When the Belly Button Pops, the Baby's Done: A Month-By-Month Guide to Surviving (and Loving) Your Pregnancy (Lorilee Craker and Juanita Moses)

Premarriage / Engagement

10 Great Dates Before You Say 'I Do' (David Arp, Claudia Arp, Curt Brown and Natelle Brown)

101 Questions to Ask Before You Get Engaged (H. Norman Wright)

Before You Plan Your Wedding . . . Plan Your Marriage (Dr. Greg Smalley, Erin Smalley and Steve Halliday)

Before You Say "I Do" (H. Norman Wright and Wes Roberts)

How Can I Be Sure? Questions to Ask Before You Get Married (Bob Phillips)

Saving Your Marriage Before It Starts: Seven Questions to Ask Before—And After—You Marry (Les Parrott and Leslie Parrott)

Rape

Forgiving the Dead Man Walking: Only One Woman Can Tell the Entire Story (Debbie Morris and Gregg Lewis)

Little Girl Lost: One Woman's Journey Beyond Rape (Leisha Joseph and Deborah Bruner Mendenhall)

When Violence Is No Stranger (Kristen J. Leslie)

Sex Industry

Dancing for the Devil: One Woman's Dramatic and Divine Rescue from the Sex Industry (Anny Donewald and Carrie Gerlach Cecil)

Scars and Stilettos: The Transformation of an Exotic Dancer (Harmony Dust)

Sexual Abuse/Assault

Beyond Our Control: Restructuring Your Life After Sexual Assault (Leila Rae Sommerfeld)

Breathe: Finding Freedom to Thrive in Relationships After Childhood Sexual Abuse (Nicole Braddock Bromley)

Caring for Sexually Abused Children: A Handbook for Families and Churches (Dr. R. Timothy Kearney)

Helping Victims of Sexual Abuse: A Sensitive Biblical Guide for Counselors, Victims, and Families (Lynn Heitritter and Jeanette Vought)

Hush: Moving from Silence to Healing After Childhood Sexual Abuse (Nicole Braddock Bromley)

Lord, I Want to Be Whole: The Power of Prayer and Scripture in Emotional Healing (Stormie Omartian)

No Longer Alone: Rising Above Childhood Sexual Abuse (Sallie Culbreth)

Slavery / Human Trafficking

Not for Sale: The Return of the Global Slave Trade—And How We Can Fight It (David Batstone)

Why Not Today: Trafficking, Slavery, the Global Church . . . and You (Matthew Cork and Kenneth Kemp)

Stress

Crazy Busy: A (Mercifully) Short Book about a (Really) Big Problem (Kevin DeYoung)

In Search of Balance: Keys to a Stable Life (Richard A. Swenson)

Juggling Chainsaws on a Tightrope: On Stress (Tim McLaughlin, Jared Lee and Arvid Wallen)

Margin: Restoring Emotional, Physical, Financial, and Time Reserves to Overloaded Lives (Richard A. Swenson)

Practice of the Presence of God (Brother Lawrence)

Stopping Stress Before It Stops You: A Game Plan for Every Mom (Kevin Leman)

Suffering / Pain

A Bend in the Road: Finding God When Your World Caves in (David Jeremiah)

A Path Through Suffering: Discovering the Relationship Between God's

Mercy and Our Pain (Elisabeth Elliot)

A Place of Healing: Wrestling with the Mysteries of Suffering, Pain, and God's Sovereignty (Joni Eareckson Tada)

Being Well When We're Ill: Wholeness and Hope in Spite of Infirmity (Marva J. Dawn)

Don't Waste Your Sorrows: Finding God's Purpose in the Midst of Pain (Paul E. Billheimer)

Holding Out for a Hero: A New Spin on Hebrews [With DVD] (Lisa Harper)

Hope for the Troubled Heart: Finding God in the Midst of Pain (Billy Graham)

How to Handle Adversity (Charles F. Stanley)

Prayers of Hope for the Brokenhearted (Jill Kelly)

The Gift of Pain: Why We Hurt and What We Can Do about It (Dr. Paul Brand and Philip Yancey)

The God of All Comfort: Devotions of Hope for Those Who Chronically Suffer (Judy Gann)

The Problem of Pain (C. S. Lewis)

Trusting God: Even When Life Hurts (Jerry Bridges)

When God Doesn't Heal Now (Larry Keefauver)

When God Weeps: Why Our Sufferings Matter to the Almighty (Joni Eareckson Tada and Steven Estes)

When I Lay My Isaac Down: Unshakable Faith in Unthinkable Circumstances (Carol Kent)

Where Is God When It Hurts? (Philip Yancey)

Suicide

Finding Your Way After the Suicide of Someone You Love (David B. Biebel and Suzanne L. Foster)

Grieving a Suicide: A Loved One's Search for Comfort, Answers and Hope (Albert Y. Hsu)

Life, in Spite of Me: Extraordinary Hope After a Fatal Choice (Kristen Jane Anderson and Tricia Goyer)

Standing in the Shadow: Help and Encouragement for Suicide Survivors (June Cerza Kolf)

Thoughts of Suicide (Josh McDowell and Ed Stewart)

Theology / Spirituality / Doctrine

Angels (Billy Graham)

Basic Christianity (John Stott)

Basic Theology: A Popular Systematic Guide to Understanding Biblical Truth (Charles Caldwell Ryrie)

Chosen by God (R. C. Sproul)

Christ Plays in Ten Thousand Places: A Conversation in Spiritual Theology (Eugene H. Peterson)

Doctrine of Repentance (Thomas Watson)

Erasing Hell: What God Said about Eternity, and the Things We Made Up (Francis Chan and Preston Sprinkle)

Essential Truths of the Christian Faith (R. C. Sproul)

Forgotten God: Reversing Our Tragic Neglect of the Holy Spirit (Francis Chan and Danae Yankoski)

Foundations of the Christian Faith (James Montgomery Boice)

Institutes of the Christian Religion (John Calvin and Henry Beveridge)

Know What You Believe (Paul E. Little)

Orthodoxy (G. K. Chesterton)

Systematic Theology: An Introduction to Biblical Doctrine (Wayne A. Grudem)

The Attributes of God (Arthur W. Pink)

The Existence and Attributes of God, Volume 7 of 50 Greatest Christian Classics, 2 Volumes in 1 (Stephen Charnock)

The Faith: What Christians Believe, Why They Believe It, and Why It Matters (Charles Colson and Harold Fickett)

The Holiness of God (R. C. Sproul)

The Sovereignty of God (Arthur W. Pink)

War / Pacifism / Violence / Evil

Chain Reaction: A Call to Compassionate Revolution (Darrell Scott and Steve Rabey)

Evil and the Justice of God (N. T. Wright)

Kids Who Kill (Mike Huckabee and George Grant)

She Said Yes: The Unlikely Martyrdom of Cassie Bernall (Misty Bernall)

Unspeakable: Facing Up to the Challenge of Evil (Os Guinness)

Why Does God Allow War? (Martyn Lloyd-Jones)

Women's Issues

Captivating: A Guided Journal to Aid in Unveiling the Mystery of a Woman's Soul (John Eldredge and Staci Eldredge)

Captivating: Unveiling the Mystery of a Woman's Soul (John Eldredge and Staci Eldredge)

For Women Only: What You Need to Know about the Inner Lives of Men (Shaunti Feldhahn)

For Young Women Only: What You Need to Know about How Guys Think (Shaunti Feldhahn and Lisa A. Rice)

Smart Women Know When to Say No (Kevin Leman)

The Allure of Hope: God's Pursuit of a Woman's Heart (Jan Meyers)

The Wounded Woman (Steve Stephens and Pam Vredevelt)

PUBLICATIONS

Fort Washington, PA 19034

This book is published by CLC Publications, an outreach of CLC Ministries International. The purpose of CLC is to make evangelical Christian literature available to all nations so that people may come to faith and maturity in the Lord Jesus Christ. We hope this book has been life changing and has enriched your walk with God through the work of the Holy Spirit. If you would like to know more about CLC, we invite you to visit our website:
www.clcusa.org

To know more about the remarkable story of the founding of CLC International we encourage you to read

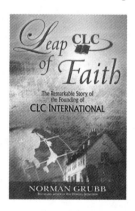

LEAP OF FAITH

Norman Grubb

Paperback
Size 5¹/₄ x 8, Pages 249
ISBN: 978-087508-650-7 - $11.99
ISBN (*e-book*): 978-1-61958-055-8 - $9.99